LIVE RICH

Other Books by Barry Kaye

$2.7 Million In My First Year

How To Save A Fortune On Your Life Insurance

Save A Fortune On Your Estate Taxes

Die Rich and Tax Free

LIVE RICH

BY

BARRY KAYE

WITH

RHONDA MORSTEIN

DOVE
BOOKS

ISBN 0-7871-1046-9

Printed in the United States of America

Dove Books
301 North Cañon Drive
Beverly Hills, CA 90210

Distributed by Penguin USA

Text design by Stanley S. Drate/Folio Graphics Co., Inc.

First Printing: March 1996

10   9   8   7   6   5   4   3   2   1

DEDICATED TO
MY GREATEST TREASURES:
MY BELOVED WIFE
CAROLE,
MY LOVING CHILDREN,
THEIR WONDERFUL SPOUSES,
AND
MY DARLING GRANDCHILDREN,
WHO HAVE TRULY MADE MY
LIFE RICH.

ACKNOWLEDGMENTS

On my last three books, *Save a Fortune on Your Life Insurance*, *Save a Fortune on Your Estate Taxes*, and *Die Rich and Tax Free*, Rhonda Morstein served as contributing editor and demonstrated a valuable and remarkable ability to take difficult, technical concepts and use her considerable writing skills to render them clear, concise, and easy to understand.

For this book, Rhonda's involvement was extended and she served with me as a cowriter, contributing her own experiences, knowledge, and materials, as well as her writing talent, to the creation of *Live Rich*.

With each new project we undertake together, Rhonda continues to impress and delight me. Her quick grasp of my intent, her ability to express that intent in words, her talent for allegory and metaphor, for speaking in the voice of common need and desire, and for using words to paint whole vistas of images and concepts have all been invaluable to this project. Her involvement has enriched this book to a far greater extent than my mere words of appreciation can express.

I would also like to acknowledge my friend and associate, Len Forman, for his steadfast support and guidance during the years of our association.

My sincere appreciation goes to Arlene Davidson as well, for the cover design and for all she does for my wife Carole and me on behalf of our Museum of Miniatures and of Barry Kaye Associates.

Finally, I want to acknowledge the works and contributions of Norman Vincent Peale, Napoleon Hill, Clement Stone, Robert Schuller, Zig Ziglar, Robert Lowe, Anthony Robbins, Billy Graham, Maxwell Maltz, Harvey MacKay, and all those who paved the path of the personal growth field. They certainly have had a positive effect on millions of people across the globe, including myself. I hope this book will add a new dimension to the good works they have already done.

CONTENTS

Contents

IT WORKED
FOR HIM

I t's fashionable to hate lawyers. And used-car salesmen are perennial favorites for the most loathed professionals. Postal employees and people who work in the motor vehicle departments and unemployment offices across the nation tolerate their share of denigration as well.

But when it comes to examining people's antipathy and distrust, no professionals bear more of a burden than members of the life insurance industry.

Whether it is because people fear confronting the inevitability of their own death or simply because the purchase of life insurance policies has traditionally been an arduously technical and confusing process, life insurance salespeople have to struggle against great odds to achieve success.

That's one of the reasons why the accomplishments of Barry Kaye are so amazing and unique. In a highly demanding profession, crowded by competition and faced with every drawback and obstacle imaginable, he has risen so far above the rest as to have virtually founded his own industry.

You may be surprised to read this because it's quite possible that you've never heard of Barry Kaye. He hasn't been standing in the spotlight, hasn't been featured in the tabloids or made the talk-show rounds. His area of concentration has been considered by the traditional media to be too specialized to capture broad appeal. And maybe that's true.

But while the rest of the world wasn't looking, Barry Kaye has published three books on the subjects of life insurance and estate-tax preservation and optimization, one of which has the distinction of being the all-time best-seller on its subject. His books are considered by many to be the definitive works within his area of expertise, and his ideas are copied and utilized by life insurance people everywhere. He's personally sold more than three billion dollars' worth of product, and he has founded a national organization that has boasted more than fifty affiliate offices across the country.

Fifty years ago, Barry Kaye became a radio and television personality in Baltimore, New York, Miami, Philadelphia, Pittsburgh, and Los Angeles. Since then he has, with the loving help and support of his wife and family, helped create the seven-trillion-dollar Wealth Creation, Preservation, and Optimization industry. He heads one of the largest, most successful life insurance operations in the country; his business generates over a hundred phone-in leads per day, and thousands of people have attended the up to one hundred seminars he gives each year. Now, Barry has appeared on national TV news programs and been featured in many newspaper and magazine articles. He's been named in *Who's Who in America* and *Who's Who in Finance and Industry* and has been a leader in his industry year after year. His clients include the rich, the political, the famous, and the powerful.

He has been involved in four careers, starting as a radio and television personality, then going on to become the head of a thriving financial business, the author of four hardcover books and two paperbacks, and, with his wife, proprietor of the Carole and Barry Kaye Museum of Miniatures in Los Angeles.

There are no professional honors he has not earned, no awards he has not been given, no position he desired that he has not attained.

Along the way, Mr. Kaye has amassed a significant personal estate; there is no arguing with his financial achievement. That achievement has allowed Mr. Kaye to enjoy the best life has to offer in all regards. But in no area does he count himself more fortunate than in his wonderful family life.

In an era of ever-increasing divorce rates and the disintegration of the nuclear family, Barry Kaye has again achieved distinctive success.

He has been married to his wife Carole for thirty-four years, and the two of them remain as devoted and inseparable now as they were when they first wed. Together they founded and own the Carole and Barry Kaye Museum of Miniatures, which they have tirelessly developed into the largest museum of contemporary miniatures in the world. Drawing upon Barry's broad vision for a unique world-class museum, Carole visualized each and every aspect of that museum and made it a reality that she administers as curator. Together they have built it into a prosperous, successful museum that delights visitors from all over the world who come to view its extraordinary collection and exhibits.

Family unity extends through all levels of the Kaye clan. Barry's sons and daughter are all a part of his business. They work side by side to build the empire that will become their legacy. All of which comes to a sudden halt, even if just for a brief moment, should one of Barry's grandchildren stop by for a visit.

Barry Kaye is a noted philanthropist who has been honored by numerous schools and foundations for his charitable and educational efforts. He has donated the media center to the American College in Bryn Mawr, Pennsylvania, in addition to having bestowed the largest endowment in the college's history. He has given a Chair to the Ben-Gurion University in Israel and has funded the Carol and Barry Kaye Mall in Beer Sheva. He has served on the boards of hospitals, schools, and other philanthropic organizations. His giving has provided a major fulfillment in his life; it is one of the great acts that contribute to his sense of living a truly rich life.

If anyone can be said to be living rich, it is Barry Kaye. Socially, professionally, personally, financially . . . he has come from nowhere to make every dream he ever had come true, in abundance.

Building upon a remarkable series of introspections that he first developed in a flood of insight when he was but fourteen years old (see Appendices 1 through 5), Barry Kaye has crafted a whole philosophy of life and applied that philosophy with a singlemindedness of purpose few can match. That purpose was to realize his fullest potential. To burst through life and arrive at its conclusion in a grand manner without having to compromise his mind, body, or spirit along the way. That he has done so cannot be argued.

Now, in this book, Barry Kaye shares with you the techniques and philosophies he has used and developed throughout his lifetime, his methods and means for achieving unparalleled personal success. Here are the keys to living rich so that you, too, might unlock the potential that exists within you and achieve whatever success you most dearly desire.

As he sums up so eloquently in the piece entitled *Then This I Say on Living Rich* (page 193), Barry Kaye's vision of the world revolves around a concept of personal achievement, integrity, and fulfillment. Of living richly and without regret. Of following one's own path while applauding others who do the same. His is a system for achieving a wholeness of self, the attainment of which makes every moment of life a rich and rewarding one.

—MICHAEL VINER
President and CEO
Dove Audio, Inc.

FROM THE AUTHOR

Live Rich is a book that hopes to show that wealth is not only about money but also about well-being. Furthermore, it intends to show you how to have a rich and fulfilling life. My purpose in writing this book is to help you have the fulfillment that I have enjoyed by showing you how I achieved it. The ideas contained within these pages are mine; they reflect only me. I mean no harm to anyone and hope only to open new doors, new vistas, and new areas of opinion and consideration that might be useful to you as you negotiate the trials and tribulations of your own life.

I hope you'll find this book motivational, inspirational, instructional, philosophical, and ideological. The system that I espouse for self-improvement is based on integrity, responsibility, self-respect, and self-awareness. These characteristics are then presented in specific situations with exercises and lessons you can use to learn how to apply them in your pursuit of a rich life.

This book addresses a person's desire for total personal fulfillment, for greater understanding of life and how to make it yield what is desired for business, family, personal, and financial success. It intends to demonstrate how to live more expansively, creatively, and romantically without any regret at the end of the road and without having to sacrifice oneself in the process.

I think that when you look over a life well spent, you will bask in the pleasures and accomplishments that were achieved. Nothing can be more important than making sure, when your life comes to its inevitable end, that you suffer no regret.

It is important that you establish a purpose to your life, a goal that will transcend all work and energy, a path that will take you out of yourself and allow you to tap into a greater reality. I cannot tell you how many times I have driven a car alone on the road, talking aloud and searching for answers and direction. What am I here for? *Why* am I here? There must be some purpose to my life, something beyond my perception. How, I wonder, will I make my mark, serve my fellow man, create a lasting legacy of my having been here? Always I have searched to unlock the mystery of self-fulfillment and, through it, fulfillment of the greater purpose we all serve. Since I was fourteen and wrote in one expansive burst of self-examination and future expectation the commentaries on life's mysteries which appear in Appendices 1 through 5, and continuing even now, I have been on this quest.

And I have discovered many things along the way. Things that have enriched my life in uncountable ways. Things that fill me with purpose and joy and fulfillment. It is these things that I want to share with you in this book. The tools and processes and philosophies and ideologies that have motivated, sustained, energized, and enlivened me.

First and foremost, I have learned that if you want something, you must go out and get it. Earn it, achieve it. Become it. Examine what you want and why you want it so you don't pursue a hollow dream—and when you find the true dreams, go after them with a vengeance.

There is no deep secret to success. No hidden mystery. In

truth, the key I've found is a simple one. I live, eat, and breathe my passions. I immerse myself in my goals. The pursuit of each new dream is a philosophy, a way of life. It's my vocation, my avocation, my hobby, and my recreation. It's a driving compulsion to succeed, to be of service to others, to make the most of my abilities. It is a complete and dedicated application of my imagination and creativity in visualizing my goal and translating the vision to reality.

These are the things that made me successful. Only with this type of feeling and dedication and focus can you become successful, if that is what you desire. If you do, and you are willing to approach that desire with your heart filled and your energy unbounded and your enthusiasm unbridled, you almost certainly will achieve success.

There is a sameness to success, for all those who have succeeded. It is as monotonous in its way as the boredom of failure. It's on display for all who wish to see it, emulate it, and be successful. Yet, although many people look at it, few see it. The pattern is even more pronounced than is the mold for failure. It is easier to be successful than to be a failure, for being successful is doing the right thing. It is easier to perform in the right manner than to incorrectly do the job. Doing it right creates its own fuel of enthusiasm and the desire to continue doing it right so that success occurs before the effort is really felt. Failing takes a toll so dire and depleting that barely enough energy remains to go on.

So if you really desire success, all you have to do is desire it enough. Enough to make its achievement your passion and your life. Enough to risk rejection, to risk failure, to invest in yourself, to buck the system, to put yourself first. It is my hope that you will find something on the following pages that will help you to focus and define your desires; ideas that motivate and teach you how to make those desires a reality every day of your life. My goal is to share with you what I have learned, to contribute any wisdom I have gained along my journey to your quest to live rich.

Vivre riche . . . Viva Ricco . . . Viva Rico . . . Leve Rig . . . Mabuhay Mayaman . . . Abril Harusd . . . Ola Waiwai . . . Lebe Reich . . . Zyi Bogaty . . . Viva Rico . . . Leve Rik . . . Hidup Kaya . . . Zengin Yasa . . . Viv Rich . . . Viu Bogat . . . Leb Reich . . . Žit' Bohatý . . . Elää Rikas . . . Leven Rijk . . . Élö Gazdag . . . Zivjeti Bogat . . . Bo Rik . . . Zyi Bogaty . . . Zistan Servatmand . . . Lichiot Ashir . . . Osheiawaseni . . . Fu Yu

In any language, in every place, throughout all time, each person who has ever lived has had a desire, an ambition, a drive to live fully and grandly and without regret. It is constant, it is universal. It is all of us and it is you. Live Rich. Achieve the dream.

IT

CAN

WORK

FOR

YOU

Living Rich

The client sitting across the desk from me put down her pen and said thoughtfully, "You know, Barry, what you always say—that we're going to be dead a lot longer than we'll be alive—is so true. I'm glad to be making these plans in accordance with your last book so I can 'die rich and tax free.' I'm happy to know I'll live on through my legacy to my children. But I've got time yet, and I don't just want to die rich—I want to *live* rich. Why haven't you got a plan that can help me do that?" Though she was laughing wryly, there was an edge of seriousness in her voice.

This person was the first of many to ask me the same question. After the publication of my book, *Die Rich and Tax Free*, I was frequently told, "Dying rich is great, Barry, but first I want to live rich! Why can't you write a book teaching people how to do that?" It occurred to me that these people were asking for more than a means to achieve financial security; that was something most of them already enjoyed. And they'd learned the lesson that wealthy people everywhere have been learning throughout the ages: Money alone does not buy happiness; wealth is best measured in more intangible terms. While money may allow you to lead a rich life, it does not necessarily enrich you.

Living rich, they generally learn, is not about wealth per se. It is about well-being. It is about grandly fulfilling all the myriad potentials and desires of which each human spirit is capable.

Living rich is characterized first by the love of family and friends. It comes from earning professional and social respect and position. It requires the fulfillment of personal goals and interests. And it includes the achievement of business success and financial independence. A richly lived life is a *big* life, filled to the brim with experience and personal satisfaction and love. It is a grand adventure, a series of dreams come true.

As I sat and pondered the need that drove people to ask me about living rich, an elderly couple I knew came to mind. The man had been very successful in business, and he and his wife were worth a significant amount of money. Yet now they were old and sick, and though they would leave their children and grandchildren a legacy of financial comfort, they had many regrets about the things they hadn't done. The man, so busy building his business and amassing his fortune, had never really had time for his family. The woman, who had surrounded herself with beautiful things, had never made the pilgrimage to Israel that she had so dearly desired. Sadly, for all their money, they had not lived rich. They epitomized the distinction between wealth and enrichment.

I knew another man, a client, who had used the wealth he'd achieved to indulge his every desire. He traveled the world, wore the finest clothes, drank fine wines, generously supported several charities, and lived in every way an expansive and gregarious life. Yet he was alone. He had always been so busy pursuing his own satisfaction that he had ultimately driven away three wives and become distant from his children. Now he was old and facing death alone. He, too, had not lived a rich life.

I wondered what these people would have told others who asked them about life's secrets. I knew they were all embittered by their regrets, and it saddens me still to think about the advantages they had and how they had wasted them. They'd lost track of what was really important, had mistaken the amassing of wealth and its unrestrained expenditure for living richly.

Yet there is no denying that financial security is an important element in living rich. Realistically, in our society it is wealth that helps provide the freedom to satisfy one's other desires. It is a very necessary means to a far more important end.

A woman I know endured a very devastating loss: Her father and her husband died, suddenly and in unrelated circumstances, three days apart from each other. In fact, she had just returned to her mother's home following her father's funeral when she received word of her husband's death. Needless to say, the emotional blow was horrific. But some time later this woman said to me, "Barry, I think sometimes of how fortunate my family was. At least we have the financial resources to sustain us through this loss we've endured. My children will not have to leave college and abandon their career goals, I do not have to worry about losing my house and surviving on Social Security. We can concentrate on trying to heal emotionally, free from the added burden of trying to survive the financial blow of losing a primary wage earner. I think of all the families who do not have this luxury and I feel, in a strange way, very lucky indeed."

No amount of money could protect this good woman and her family from their tragic loss. But financial security made it easier for them to focus on what was truly important: grieving, honoring their loss, and pulling together as a family. So it is, though in exact reverse, with wealth and living rich. No amount of money can buy happiness, but having money makes it easier to pursue that which makes you happy and does enhance your options.

Which is not to say that happiness is impossible without wealth; that is obviously not the case. But the concept of living rich as I have espoused it goes beyond just being happy or satisfied with one's life, it goes beyond making the best of what is available. To live rich is to possess the means for making life provide all that you desire of it.

But what are those means? If wealth alone does not ensure a richly lived life, what does?

The means, I realized, are the same no matter what the goal. Whether your desire is great wealth or professional esteem or fame, or whether what you are really after is a great love or personal achievement, the means to achieving the end are always the same.

Mostly the answer lies in your attitude and personal philosophy. In dedicating yourself to your goal with a single-mindedness of purpose. In maintaining a sharp focus on your desired end and refusing to be swayed by the many forces that work to drag all of us down into mediocrity.

There are many more followers than leaders in this world. There are many more people who accept the status quo than who have the vision to rise above it. There are far more individuals who fear change than who work to create it. And there is a large majority who have simply abdicated responsibility for their lives. These people will never live rich. Worse, they will often try to stop you from doing so in order to justify their own mediocrity. They will decry your attempts as being vain and self-absorbed. They will erect barriers and obstacles. They will insist you live down to their level.

But if you want to live rich, you must first and foremost resist the siren call of their promised security and acceptance. You must be your own person and believe wholeheartedly in the value of your own dreams and goals. Without this fierce desire and self-assurance, you cannot fulfill yourself. No follower ever made more of himself than those he followed. Remember, in the Iditarod dog-sled race, only the lead dog enjoys a full view and has a change of scenery.

In my business, I now have many associates across the country. These salespeople use my materials and techniques, they follow my formulas and strategies, they utilize my methods and approaches. Most of them make very nice livings. Some of them do extremely well. But none does as well as I do, because I receive some part of all the business that I refer to them or that they bring in using my name and programs. This is fair, as they are profiting from the risks I took initially, the programs I developed, the innovations I created, the investments I made. By following my own vision I have accelerated their success, and in so doing enhanced my own success manyfold. Had I simply followed the accepted courses that were my industry's standards when I began, had I been content not to risk rocking the boat or bucking the accepted way of doing things, few of my achievements would have been possible.

The same is true in virtually every self-made success story out there. From captains of industry to star athletes to the president himself, the single greatest commonality fueling their achievement is their will. Their drive. Their focus.

Does that mean that only those rare people born with an extraordinary will can achieve the personal success of a richly lived life? No. We all have will and desire and purpose. They exist within each and every one of us. But some people are better at applying their will than others. Often our will is negated by circumstances. Perhaps neglectful parents or other childhood factors have softened our resolve or made us question the value of our dreams or our ability to attain them. Perhaps we've been beaten down by failure. Or perhaps we're held back by the envy of others who try to sabotage our success to make their own failure seem less onerous. Maybe it is just that some people have a more highly evolved internal knowledge of how best to apply their will. Maybe there are prodigies, not unlike the musical and mathematical geniuses who crop up every now and again, who simply know how to tap into the well of their will. For them, achievement seems to come easily. But that doesn't mean it is impossible for those who weren't born with some unique gift or weren't raised in an extremely nurturing environment to learn to harness the remarkable power of their own will.

Fortunately, the exercise of will is something that can be learned and taught. There are methods and practices that strengthen a person's ability to apply and devote himself or herself. Ways to forge, nurture, and develop the skills that turn a desire for success into that success.

A friend of mine had a grandson who was smaller and less developed than the other children his age. In sports and athletic endeavors he was always being left behind. But, oh, how he wanted to play and compete!

The boy threw himself into each new challenge with all his heart and soul. He wasn't afraid to work toward his goal, to give his all toward its achievement. Yet even so, time and again he did not make the cut.

Then a new coach came to the boy's school. This coach, seeing the youngster's drive and determination, took him under his wing. He showed the boy better ways to apply his will and taught him new techniques of discipline. Rather than having the boy try to match strength he could not equal, the coach showed him how to use his speed and agility to the best advantage; to make the most of his own attributes and not waste time applying himself to things he could not control.

With work, the boy blossomed and achieved his goals. He had learned how to best apply his will, how to weave realities from the fabric of his dreams. These are lessons that are available to everyone.

Will, and the determined, knowledgeable exercise of will. These are the common themes in virtually every success story there is.

When George Foreman announced that, at age forty-five, he would fight then–heavyweight champion Michael Moorer for the title, reactions ranged from stunned disbelief to astonishment to snickering. Here, indeed, was a dreamer's dream. But Foreman possessed an uncommon will to win; the mature ability to assess his own strengths, weaknesses, and potentials; and the knowledge of how to train effectively. Mr. Foreman knocked out his opponent in the tenth round and claimed a title he had not been able to take from Muhammad Ali twenty years earlier.

George Foreman can surely be said to be living rich. He dared a dream and achieved it. He refused to accept the restrictions others would have placed around his goals—he defied the very concept of limitations. And he won that which meant the most to him. *That* is living rich.

It is my belief that anyone can do the same. Anyone with the desire and willingness—and *willfulness*—to apply himself can achieve the personal wealth of a fulfilled life. All it takes is the drive, and knowledge of the best techniques for focusing and applying that drive.

Love It or Leave It

You've heard it said a million times that "love is a harsh mistress." And it's certainly true. Love is the most demanding and challenging activity we humans engage in. But I've always thought of it from the other side: When pursuing a dream that is consuming and rigorous, you'd better love it.

No matter how great your will, how lofty your dream, how extensive your training, if you do not love the course you are following, success is almost impossible to achieve. The devotion necessary to achieve your goal becomes drudgery if you don't love what you do. The time required becomes time resented instead of time enjoyed. The joy of a consuming passion is replaced with the bitterness of a consuming burden. In these conditions, your ability to bring to bear the imagination, vitality, and determination necessary for success becomes greatly limited. Faced with an unappealing task day after day, no matter how great your desire for the rewards of its completion, you cannot help but become slug-gish and embittered in its pursuit.

Even if you are able to push your way through the obsta-cles and achieve the final goal toward which your efforts have been directed, the price you have to pay will eat up any reward. You will not be living rich, for you will have sacri-ficed days, years, perhaps a lifetime of unhappiness and drudgery for a single moment or measure of success that will inevitably seem shallow and empty at the end.

Think of Dan Jansen skating in Olympic competition after competition in pursuit of a gold medal and meeting with one tragic failure after another, one public disappoint-ment after another. Imagine what his course would have been like if Dan didn't love skating, if he didn't thrive on the training and the discipline and the challenge. Could a greed for Olympic gold alone have seen him through the heart-breaks, the years of hard work, the emotional strain? By all accounts, what kept Dan going was his love of skating and his love of his family. These are what gave him the will and strength to endure and eventually triumph. And what would his gold medal have been worth had it represented only a resented, wasted life? If he'd pursued his dream with bitter need instead of joy, would that moment we all watched as he skated his victory lap with his daughter in his arms and tears in his eyes have been so poignant or delicious? Wouldn't it, instead, have been hollow and drained of pleasure?

It is the same with any dream. If you don't love the *process* of the goal's achievement, the reward is negated by the cost of its attainment.

I remember the day a man came into my office to discuss some plans for the dispersal of his estate after his death. He was a powerful man, quick of speech and abruptly decisive. He approached our conversation with a vengeance, growling and gesticulating fiercely. Slowly the story emerged. The man had worked his whole life at a job he'd disliked because he thought it was his premier responsibility to provide a good life for his heirs. Now he'd achieved the goal and would leave a tidy sum behind. But he'd given up so much for that dream, had grown so embittered of his sacrifice, that there was no joy in the accomplishment. In fact, he resented his heirs for having robbed him of his life and regretted every day that he'd slaved at his business. He'd never loved the harsh mistress that drove him to succeed, and now, at the end of his life, it was too late to find the love he missed. This is not what living rich is about.

I also knew a young woman, the daughter of a couple who had built a successful family business and who had always assumed their children would take it over from them in due time. Their son, however, married and moved out of state with his wife and child. That left the daughter. She didn't really want the business but didn't know how to tell her parents and didn't feel she could turn down such a wonderful gift. After all, she told herself, it would mean financial security and professional position and independence—things she convinced herself she should want. So she gave up her dream of being a journalist and went into the family business. But though she was certainly an intelligent woman, her heart wasn't in it. She chafed at the responsibility and resented the time and energy it took. It was not long before the business was in trouble and had to be sold. No matter how much the young woman wanted to honor her parents' wishes and make them proud, the task was too hard for someone who didn't love it as they had.

We all know similar stories. The son-in-law who goes into the family business to please his wife's parents and winds up ruining his marriage with resentment and bitterness. The child actor, pushed by his parents into pursuing *their* dream, who turns into a troubled teenager whose face is plastered all over the tabloids. The woman who marries for position and security instead of love and ultimately becomes sour and tired and sad. Time and again we see it, and the lesson is crystal clear: If you don't love what you are doing, you can't make it succeed. Or, in the rare case that you do, you find that what you have is not nearly as precious as what you've lost.

Whatever your personal quest—be it wealth, position, romance, or achievement—the demands will be as grueling as the reward is big. If you want to become successful in business you must be prepared to work long hours, to be the first one into the office and last one to leave, to take the job with you everywhere you go.

Do you want to forgo the rigors and demands of the business world and make your fortune playing the stock market? Fine. Be ready to awaken each day before dawn to know what's happening in the world markets before Wall Street opens. Know that you will have to stay tuned to your computer's stock quotation program throughout the day, breaking only to read the financials and analyze movement.

Maybe you think you'll make your fortune as a doctor. After all, the good ones are paid very well. Of course, you'll have to complete years of schooling, do a residency that is reported to be one of the most physically challenging stresses imaginable, and struggle in an internship. Then you'll need to be prepared to be available at all hours, to sacrifice your home life, your recreation, your sleep to the needs of your patients.

But perhaps it isn't money that you're after. Perhaps what you really want is fame. I read an interesting account of Daniel Day-Lewis's preparation for the role of disabled artist Christy Brown in the movie *My Left Foot*, for which he won his first Oscar. It seems that in order to best portray the character, Day-Lewis spent eight weeks in a wheelchair at a Dublin palsy clinic learning to type, write, and paint with his left foot. In fact, his regimen was so grueling that by the end of the movie's filming two of his vertebrae had to be realigned.

What is really remarkable about this story is that it is not unusual. Ask any truly successful actor, athlete, musician, artist, or writer about what they have had to go through and you will hear a similar tale.

Even if your goal is as seemingly simple and uncomplicated as finding a life partner, falling in love, and living a life of shared happiness and joy, you will not escape or avoid challenge and rigorous demands.

We often hear about how difficult it is to meet compatible people in today's fast, complicated world. A widow of my acquaintance missed being part of a couple, missed having a partner. Unfortunately, especially at her age, the number of available men was greatly overshadowed by the number of available women. This woman joined several dating services, attended singles parties and functions, joined the country club, and signed up for arranged games of bridge and of mixed doubles tennis. Every time I saw her she was dressed impeccably, and when I complimented her on that fact she told me she couldn't afford not to look her best every moment of the day in the event that she might meet someone in an unexpected fashion. It was tiring, she confided, and sometimes she wished she could just throw on something comfortable, forget the makeup, and let her hair down, but the effort would be worth it if it led to a new love.

Nor is this difficulty reserved for the older segment of our population. The young, too, face many difficulties in finding something as basic as love. Young professionals, consumed with building a career, have little time to meet and socialize, and less time still to date and court and do the hard work of getting to know each other.

Even when love is found, the work is not over, it has only begun. Ask any successful couple and they will tell you there is no harder job than being a partner to someone else. It takes devotion and time and energy, patience and compromise, and a willingness to listen and talk and yell and cry and hug. And that's just to sustain a marriage or romance; *just wait* until there are children!

The point is, there is no endeavor and no reward without its rigor and its hardship. There is nothing you can pursue, no goal or dream you can achieve, without a cost. Paying that price, virtually with your life, is something you should only do out of love for the harsh mistress.

"You know what, Barry?" the attractive sixty-five-year-old widow whispered to me in the voice of a giddy girl, as we discussed her devoted search for a man, "I really love the whole thing," she stated. "I love dating, meeting new men, being taken out and spoiled a bit, dressing up and being admired. To tell you the truth, it's fun!" I knew she'd be fine. Interestingly, her daughter, a lovely, accomplished, charming thirty-year-old woman, was single and had never been married. She was with us in the meeting and I turned to her and asked, "What about you? No man in your life?" She sighed. "I'd like there to be. But I hate the whole process. Dating is a drag, a chore. Most of the men are selfish or boring or afraid of commitment. I hate dressing up for them as if I were a piece of merchandise to be assessed and compared. It's all so superficial." That was about five years ago. The mother has since remarried. She and her new husband are very happy. The daughter is still single.

When you do what you love doing just for the sake of the enjoyment of it, you can often be surprised by the end result.

My wife, Carole, began collecting miniatures about six years ago. She loved the delicate pieces of furniture, loved arranging the model homes, delighted in the intricacy and realism that could be achieved. Over the years, Carole acquired new pieces and developed new displays. Each one brought her a new joy and a new sense of accomplishment. In pursuit of her pleasure, she studied other collections, haunted specialty shops, visited museums, talked to experts, read up on the subject, and made phone calls all over the globe through which she learned that her collection was well on the way to becoming one of the largest in the world. We smiled at that idea—it was a fun thought—and Carole kept on doing what she'd loved doing all along.

Today, Carole and I own the largest museum of contemporary miniatures in the world, based in Los Angeles not far from the headquarters of my business. Our *Museum of Miniatures* is visited by over one hundred thousand people a year and has been written about in *The New York Times*, the *Los Angeles Times*, and newspapers worldwide. The museum features some of the most noteworthy displays of their type.

"But where do you get the energy for all this?" is the question I am most frequently asked by people who desire to achieve what Carole and I have achieved. The only answer I have ever been able to think of is that it comes naturally. I love my business. I relish each day of it. If there is one single secret to my success, surely that is it. The aggravations are challenges, the setbacks new opportunities, the achievements themselves are incidental to the process of achieving. I love that my success allows me to spoil my grandchildren, permits me to support the causes that I believe are important. My life is often frenetic, my days start early and end late, the demands placed upon me seem endless. And all of it would add up to an unbearable degree of pressure and stress if it were not for that one simple truth: I love my life, I love what I do, I would not choose to be doing anything else.

Think about something in your life that you love to do. Even if it is something simple, like walking the dog, or gardening, or cooking. You don't have to create energy to do those things. It is simply there. In fact, those activities may seem to create an energy of their own. They invigorate you. So it is with any endeavor. I do not have to "find" the energy to run my business, Carole does not have to "find" the energy to run the museum, neither of us has to "find" the energy to nurture our family. These are things we love to do; they invigorate us. And that is the basic how and why of our success.

So think about something you love to do, find inside yourself that charged, excited, invigorated feeling that you get when you are doing it. Then assess the dreams and goals that you are pursuing in your life. Do you get the same feeling? Does the mere thought of engaging in the activity charge and invigorate you? If it does, you are probably well on your way to a successful and richly lived life. If it doesn't, you should probably think about reassessing that goal. Life is too short and achievement too harsh a mistress to spend it doing anything less than something you love.

"Do what you love," the saying goes, "and the money will come." Maybe, maybe not. But it isn't really important. I say, love it or leave it. If it doesn't make you happy each and every day, you're not doing right by yourself or those you are working for or working with. I can't emphasize this point too strongly: Love what you are doing and you are already rich.

Don't Be a Victim of "Conventional Wisdom"

According to biblical accounts, in about 2000 B.C. a man named Abraham living in a place called Ur in Mesopotamia came to see as false gods the many idols and deities that his people worshipped. He was the first person to come to a belief in a single god, and he desired to enlighten all the people in his region to his discovery.

In his attempts to demonstrate the false nature of the people's reverence for their sculpted idols, it is said that Abraham destroyed the statues, hoping to show how frail and vulnerable and "ungodlike" they were. Instead, he earned his people's wrath. They were unable to embrace the new idea, unable to give up what they had been taught and had placed their faith in. Reviled and cast out as a heretic, Abraham and his family went to the land of Canaan, where they ultimately changed the course of history.

Today Abraham is credited with having forever altered

man's relationship with his world and his God. He is revered as the patriarch of the three great monotheistic religions: Judaism, Christianity, and Islam.

In the early 1600s Galileo Galilei, Italian mathematician, astronomer, and physicist, became the first man to use a telescope in studying the skies. Through his observations, Galileo amassed sufficient evidence to prove that the Earth revolves around the Sun and is not the center of the universe as had previously been believed.

This position represented such a radical departure from the accepted belief of the day that Galileo was tried by the Inquisition in Rome. He was ordered to recant and forced to spend the last eight years of his life under house arrest. His theories and conclusions were decried and banned.

Yet today Galileo is often referred to as the founder of modern mechanics and experimental physics, and his name is justly associated with a vast extension of the bounds of the visible universe. The myriad galaxies themselves pay tribute to his vision and accomplishment.

In 1776 a ragtag group of revolutionaries, led in battle by George Washington and in spirit by John Adams, Thomas Jefferson, and Benjamin Franklin, asserted their independence from the British Empire and demanded the freedom of self-determination.

Declaring that "all men are created equal, that they are endowed by their Creator with certain unalienable Rights, that among these are Life, Liberty and the pursuit of Happiness," these men and their compatriots in the Continental Congress flew in the face of all previously accepted political theory and ultimately formed a new government "Of the people, By the people and For the people."

It was believed at the time that the United States of America could not possibly succeed as a nation. It was "*known*" that the general population of a country did not have the ability, knowledge, or wisdom to govern itself. Yet today the only superpower remaining on earth stands tall on the foundations of those daring principles.

In 1844 Dr. Ignaz Semmelweis was appointed assistant at the obstetric clinic in Vienna. At the time of his appointment, mortality rates for delivering women ran as high as 30 percent.

It was commonly believed that the puerperal infections which killed so many of the women were induced by overcrowding, poor ventilation, the onset of lactation, or a general, nonspecific "miasma." Semmelweis investigated the cause over the objections of his chief, who, like other continental physicians of the time, had reconciled himself to the idea that the disease was unpreventable.

Semmelweis noted that the incidence of disease was higher among women treated by physicians who had just come from the dissecting rooms. These observations led him to believe that, contrary to accepted thought, the doctors must carry some disease agent from the dead bodies to the living. He ordered the doctors to wash their hands in a solution of chlorinated lime before performing an examination, and mortality rates dropped from 18 percent to 1 percent!

Though his efforts to disseminate his findings were initially met with resistance from jealous or ignorant superiors, the success of Semmelweis's measures eventually could not be ignored. There is no accurate means of counting the number of people whose lives his findings ultimately saved.

■

The success of each of these men was predicated in large part by their courageous willingness to buck the conventional wisdom of their day. In fact, the opportunities they seized were created exactly by opposition to conventional wisdom. Because it was generally accepted that the Earth was the center of the universe or disease resulted from poor ventilation, the singular person who pioneered the alternate path had automatically secured a position of leadership.

The same is true in every field of endeavor existing today. Where there is a "common wisdom" that tells you something must be done a certain way, there is an opportunity for great success. It need not be on a scale of Galileo's or Semmelweis's achievement; the chances are few and far between that a person gets to affect all of humankind in the ways that they did. But you *can* affect your personal world with the same fiery brand of free thinking. And you can earn similar results in terms of your personal success.

Common wisdom is, in my opinion, a trap that most people refuse to see and into which they willingly, blindly walk. People find safety in following the established path, even if it leads to a stagnant dead end. They like to rely on something other than their own judgment for the answers to how things should be. That way, they do not have to take responsibility for the outcome and they do not have to risk being wrong.

But the riskier the activity you undertake, the greater the reward that is available. Safety earns you nothing but more safety.

Every time you hear the words, "It'll never fly," or,

"That's not how it works," or, "It can't be done," you are being issued an invitation to achievement and success. There is a Chinese proverb that says, "The person who says it cannot be done should not interrupt the person doing it." Don't let naysayers interrupt your achievement.

When I entered the life insurance industry in 1962, I found it to be a virtual bastion of conventionally accepted thinking. There were "rules" for just about every aspect of selling: how to approach new prospects, how to advertise, how to depict the benefits of the available products, how to structure policies. But after learning all these standard methods I realized they were not based on anything other than tradition: Each new person coming into the industry was told of the standards by those who had come before. This handing down of conventional wisdom is nothing more than a means the old guard uses to justify itself to the new, and it is in place in every industry I have ever come in contact with.

I started asking, "Why?" and, when no satisfactory answer was forthcoming, wondered, "Why not?" And I began doing things my own way.

Advertising for life insurance was, at that time, bland and almost apologetic. It usually featured a somewhat melodramatic depiction of the tragedy of death as portrayed by the insurance industry: male breadwinners called to a beatific heaven concerned evermore with having left their wives and families behind to struggle along without them. The serious, tombstone typeface informed the reader that "it doesn't have to be this way."

The industry talked about death as if it were our fault. As if by selling insurance we created, or at very least endorsed, mortality and were somehow tainted by our efforts to capitalize on its presence. No wonder people were so leery of insurance salespeople; who would want to be approached by someone of this demeanor and bearing? It could only be an unpleasant experience.

But when I asked why we sabotaged ourselves like this, why we were so craven in our approaches, the only answer I got was that it was always done this way. The conventional wisdom said people would not respond to more straightforward discussions about death. I didn't believe it. I knew *I* would prefer to talk directly about the subject, knew *I* was aware of the inevitability of death, and I was pretty sure that I was not unique.

I started running ads that reflected my way of thinking. Death is going to happen, I told my prospects. You can be ready, or not.

Some people in my industry were horrified by my ads. How dare I run so blunt a headline as one that read, "You Are Going To Die!" I would ruin us all. "Six Million Dollars Tax Free," another ad proclaimed; how crass could I be, to discuss so irreverently the financial benefits of such a ghoulish product? Frankly, I enjoyed the controversy because it told me I was shaking things up in an industry that I just *knew* needed shaking up. So even though the stock market was soaring at the time, I ran an ad that announced, "The Stock Market Will Crash 2500 Points." Did it get attention? You bet it did. At first, of course, everyone thought I was crazy to make such a wild, unpopular statement. But I liked being different in pursuit of my goal. The ad copy explained my premise, and I kept selling more and more product.

In ads like those that stated, "Buy $5,000,000 for $25,000 a Year," "Increase Your $10,000 Annual Tax-Free Gift to $1,000,000," "Recover All Losses from Your Real Estate, Stock, and Business Investments," and *"Double* Your Gross Estate, *Triple* Your Net Estate," I had the gall to discuss the way life insurance could be used to optimize investment and financial portfolios. It was shocking, they said ("they" being everyone who had been too frightened, too unimaginative, or too much a victim of conventional wisdom to try the approach). The funny thing was, people responded in record numbers to the "shock" of realizing they had been missing out on such a valuable opportunity.

That the ads worked as well as they did reinforced what I'd suspected: People were receptive to truth and straight talk, they were able to comprehend the nuances of life insurance as a financial planning tool.

I ventured further and further afield from what I had been told were sacrosanct approaches to the sale of my product. I talked about forced liquidation, about pensions and IRAs and generation-skipping transfer tax exemptions, until some members of my industry fairly shrieked that I wasn't selling *life insurance* at all anymore. And I guess they were right. I certainly wasn't selling what they were.

Today I eagerly and with a somewhat devilish glee anticipate their reactions to my newest ad—the one that cuts my own throat. The one in which I call for an end to all estate taxes; the discounting of which, through the use of life insurance, is the foundation of my insurance operation.

"Estate Tax Abolished," the headline proclaims, looking forward to a day, which I hope arrives soon, when this unfair, burdensome, and costly tax is removed. "But Barry," the colleagues to whom I have shown the mockups ask in confusion, "are you crazy? Estate taxes are the backbone of your business."

Conventional wisdom would have me support something I know is detrimental to individuals and the nation in order to bolster my own business. I am too concerned for the future of my children, grandchildren, and country not to rock the boat once more. Somehow, I think it'll be a fun ride.

Interestingly, a consortium of life insurance companies has recently joined together and pooled their resources to the tune of twenty million dollars for an industry-specific ad campaign. The headlines for the first three ads they've developed are:

"You're Dead. What Do You Do Now?"
"Would You Mind Dying for a Moment?"
"Is There Life After Death?"

Sound familiar?

But my lack of convention extended beyond just the manner in which I advertised. I spoke freely about my commissions, was not ashamed to admit that I was making money selling my products. After all, the policies I sold were of great value to the people who bought them. They would provide the benefits they promised. I was not a ghoul profiting from tragedy and death; I was a professional selling a much-needed product, and I deserved to make a living doing so the same as anyone else.

People responded to my approach. They came to respect me because I respected myself. Because I spoke so directly and honestly about the hard facts of my field, they knew they could trust me to speak honestly about the policies I presented.

Of course, the pundits and authorities of the life insurance industry were appalled. This was not how it was supposed to be done! I was told over and over, in confidential meetings, by well-meaning mentors, at industry social events, that I was doing it wrong and would only alienate people. Until, of course, my success started to become publicly evident. It was difficult to argue with that. I consistently sold more product than almost all of my competitors, and in some years I led sales in as many as three or four insurance companies at the same time.

Having proven with great results that the accepted conventions of my industry were not, in fact, the great truths they were presented as being, I continued to expand my efforts. It was amazing to me how great a hole had been created by adherence to the "rules." Whole areas of opportunity had been overlooked, ignored, or discounted because the industry bought into the belief that it was somehow taboo.

In the years that followed, I tested and pushed many of the imposed limits of the life insurance industry. I lobbied the insurers for new types of policies that would better fulfill the needs of customers. I instituted new payment options previously thought to be beyond people's comprehension. I developed new usages and applications for insurance in overall financial planning.

But my most extreme success came when I discarded many of the accepted practices of my industry altogether and moved off in a wholly new direction.

Until that point, I was still primarily selling life insurance as a hedge against the unforeseen tragedy of death. To some extent I had embraced the most central, core example of my industry's conventional wisdom. Then it dawned on me: Death was not, would never be, an unforeseen tragedy. How could it be when it happens to us all? Death was a certainty, the one certainty constant to all humanity.

With this realization came the understanding that the true value of life insurance was in its use as a financial optimization and maximization tool. This unconventional insight altered my focus entirely.

I looked at the areas of life where forward financial planning was most needed and saw the tragedy of estate taxation. Almost immediately, I saw a niche that no one had ever before considered approaching in my unique manner. I saw the potential and possibilities that had been overlooked and began to move my focus to embrace them.

Life insurance is a marvelous, nearly magical estate planning tool. It accomplishes things no other financial vehicle can accomplish. Yet no one had thought to present its uses to the public from this perspective. The conventional wisdom had not embraced this direction as being viable or profitable, and no one had thought to challenge that wisdom. Which was all to my great good fortune, for the fact was that once people were shown the benefits of what life insurance could accomplish for them, they understood and accepted the concept in huge numbers. Thousands of families were saved millions of dollars, practically an entire new industry was created, a new door was opened through which countless professionals have since flocked, and, frankly, my personal fortune was greatly enhanced. Most important, I truly felt I had done my country a service, as America benefited from the optimized and maximized wealth of my clients—wealth they could then use to invest in their nation's future.

The next thing I did flew in the face of standard, accepted practices even more. The personal nature of the subject of death had led insurance salespeople to assume that the sale of their product had to occur in an individual and personal setting. "Why?" I wondered. Though surely the moment of dying is an extremely private one, the *fact* of death is the most universal truth there is. Wouldn't it be easier to talk about it and consider it in a group, removing it from the mystical dark places and bringing it into the light of reasoned consideration and planning?

Convinced that people would respond if given the chance, I began the seminars that have since made my name in the industry. Targeting those with a need for estate tax planning,

I produced seminars all over the country and began pioneering the mass marketing of life insurance products. Though none of the gurus of my industry thought it would work—many of them sternly counseled me against it, saying that "you can't possibly sell large policies on a mass marketing basis"—I have in the past ten years given over a thousand seminars, attended by tens of thousands of people. Through those seminars I have sold literally billions of dollars of product.

I recite this history not in order to brag, but for no other reason than to show what can be accomplished when a person stops following the accepted path and branches out in a pioneering new direction. The facts are what they are and speak for themselves. I am simply using them to demonstrate the power and opportunity of questioning conventional wisdom and refusing to be its victim. I do not believe myself to be so unique or special in any fundamental way. But I did have the courage to follow my own beliefs and to thwart the conventional wisdom, which would have limited my achievement to a lesser level.

In every industry, every field of endeavor, there evolves a myth of conventional wisdom. Those who blindly adhere to the restrictions will never create the breakthroughs that lead to the greatest reward. Only those who look beyond the accepted means of doing things can achieve the heights of success and personal fulfillment.

Conventional wisdom might well have dictated that Steve Forbes run his empire, mind his own business, enjoy his life, his family, and the personal success of taking *Forbes* magazine way beyond what was handed to him upon his father's death. However, with every fiber of his being Steve Forbes realized that a social responsibility called him to leave the comfort and privacy of his home, family, and business empire to pursue a higher purpose. The move was a risky one for Mr. Forbes, who was not a politician and did not have the brash, egotistical charisma that characterizes most career politicians. He is a shy, quiet man with a humbleness that is totally nonpolitical in every way. I know this because it has been my great good fortune to have been associated with Steve Forbes, and his father before him, for years.

Flying in the face of all common expectation, responding to a need he saw as urgent, fearful that the path his nation was following could lead to economic, moral, and political devastation, Steve Forbes threw his hat into the most competitive and controversial political arena there is—the race for the presidency of the United States.

Everything about Mr. Forbes's candidacy contradicted conventional wisdom. He was a complete outsider in a world as cliquish and partisan as any gets. He provided his own campaign funding. He had no political experience.

But what was particulary unusual about Steve Forbes's presidential race was the platform upon which he ran. For Steve Forbes chose to increase the distance between conventional politics and his own campaign by espousing a particularly unconventional wisdom. He defied the class-conscious, partisan politics that inspire candidates to embrace whichever side of an issue they think will garner the most support. Instead, he presented what many people are beginning to view as a commonsense, logical philosophy that extends beyond the popular, the conventional, or the convenient. Using his knowledge of economics and of business and worldwide economies, along with a formidable grasp of history, Steve Forbes embodied a political position that captured the attention and interest of people from all walks, classes, backgrounds, and professions.

Contrary to the growth of big government that has

gripped this country for decades, and in direct opposition to the unstated bureaucratic principle that seems to suggest that the people exist to serve the government instead of the other way around, Steve Forbes dared to resist the establishment. He advocated principles of responsibility and honesty and clarity that most other politicians seem to have abandoned in favor of protecting their own self-interest and espousing whatever popular view will help them get reelected.

While more conventional politicians exacerbated a class war and used taxes as the weapon that keeps various segments of the population in opposition to one another in order to capitalize on the tension, Steve Forbes advocated a flat tax. While more conventional politicians spoke half-truths that pandered to their audience's predispositions—predispositions the politicians themselves created in order to develop a segmented constituency—Steve Forbes presented the whole picture in an effort to unite and benefit all Americans. He didn't toe the popular line and support the middle class at the expense of the wealthy. He ran the risk of stating the truth and trusting the people to understand that when the rich are not overburdened and stripped of their wealth by taxes that benefit no one but the government, they are free to invest in the economy of America, to create more jobs, more opportunity, more investment capital, more prosperity for all.

Steve Forbes has made his mark. He brought to the forefront of American thinking crucial issues that had been ignored for too long. He made people think, made the media break free of its complacency and question once again the bill of fare our career politicians have been serving us. Concepts like the flat tax, which have been discussed before but never really considered, were finally looked at seriously because of Steve Forbes's support. His success in the early polls influenced the platforms of the other candidates and gave the

American people a means by which to demonstrate how fed up they are with the business-as-usual politics that are killing this country. Things will not be exactly the same again, no matter who gets elected. The career politicians have been shook up some. And that's a lot to say for the endeavor of one man—that he changed the course of this nation.

Personally, I long for the day when "partisan politics" is a dirty phrase and we can become a nation dedicated to the principles upon which we were founded. The first time I hear a news report that says, "Thanks to the signing into law of the proposed new tax reforms, Americans will enjoy new financial benefits in the future," instead of "The rich got richer today thanks to the new tax-reform bills," I will thank Steve Forbes and those like him who dared to buck the conventional wisdom and in so doing made a lasting mark on the landscape of the American dream. And on that day—could it be July 4, 1997?—I will run a new ad proclaiming the signing of the Declaration of Financial Independence, and I'll rejoice that people sometimes *do* risk everything for the benefit of others.

It is perhaps one of the greatest failures of people pursuing a goal that they do not extend themselves beyond the accepted ways of doing things. Don't be a victim of conventional wisdom. Look at what you do with a critical eye. Examine the daily assumptions you make about how things have to be done. Ask, "Why?" a lot, and if the answer you get doesn't make sense to you, it's probably because it doesn't make much sense, period. If you devise a more logical way of doing something, chances are that it will appeal to others, too. Within that knowledge lies the power of success. It takes only the concentrated and courageous exercise of your own best judgment. Experiment and try those things that have previously been thought impossible or improbable. Thwart the conventional wisdom.

Carefully examine the endeavors you engage in. Think for a minute about the assumptions that lie at the very heart of the processes you follow. Make a list of the truisms you have accepted. Now consider each one. Does it really make sense to you? Does it seem as inviolate as it is presented to be? Who benefits by your belief in it? Can you think of a better way? Remember, it used to be accepted that no one could run a four-minute mile or swim the English Channel. These limits were not imposed and accepted by those who might try and fail, however, but as an excuse for those too afraid to try.

What is the "four-minute mile" of your life? Where have you put limitations on your own potential? As surely as Roger Bannister broke that four-minute mile and in so doing set the way for many others to follow, you too can break through the invisible barriers holding you back from achieving your goals. Don't accept any limitations on your dreams. If you can conceive it, you can achieve it. Only you will make your own limitations. It is not written anywhere that you aren't entitled to reach for the stars.

Recognize the opportunities that are created when everyone flocks in a common direction; he or she who goes the other way will stand alone. And it is when you occupy a lone position that you capture the most attention and interest.

Conventional wisdom taints all aspects of human endeavor. It is present in the areas of human relationship; think, for example, about the saying, "Men don't make passes at girls who wear glasses." What is this cliche if not a passing on of conventional wisdom, the only possible outcome of which is to keep a nearsighted woman from believing herself to be desirable?

Our culture is rife with these sorts of insidious "lessons."

They permeate every niche, every field, every path of aspiration. In business they say, "It takes money to make money." But who are "they," and how many people are held back from striving for the financial success they desire because they have blindly accepted that not having money dooms them to not being able to make it? Even so, *The Wall Street Journal* abounds with stories of people who started a business with the cash advance they could charge on their credit card and who are now millionaires. Apparently, those people hadn't heard that without a bundle of capital to get started they could not succeed.

To live rich, resist the homogenization of conventional wisdom. Be less concerned with what "they" say and more concerned with your own beliefs and ideas. No matter what happens, whether you achieve your goal or not, you will at least know that you lived your life on your terms, within the parameters you created for yourself and to your own standards. This alone will make your life a rich one.

S T E P

4

Carpe Diem
(Seize the Day)

In the movie *Dead Poets Society*, there is a scene in which Robin Williams, playing an English teacher at a private boys' preparatory school, exhorts his students to expand their vision of the world and reject any common explanation of what things are or can be. To make his point, he has each of the boys climb up onto his desk to survey the room and his classmates from a new vantage. He challenges them to go through life seeking opportunities to alter their perspectives, to see things from all views, to dismiss the obvious in favor of the more rare.

It's a simple scene; there's no big dramatic moment or special effects. But I found it thrilling. The sight of one boy after another stepping up onto the desk and surveying familiar surroundings suddenly made unfamiliar and exciting by virtue of being seen from a new direction was quite moving. The look on the boys' faces as they each realized that this simple, seemingly silly little experiment was really quite portentous made me feel as if I were being given the chance to reanimate my world along with them. Their eyes were being opened to a new way of thinking. Is there anything more thrilling than that?

Carpe diem. Seize the day. This is the main theme of *Dead Poets Society* and it should become the main theme of your life. Seize every day, every hour, every moment, for each could be your last. You will be dead much longer than you will be alive; life is woefully short. As was once written, "Life is but a clap of thunder in the sky." Take a full breath every morning and thank the powers that be for the goodness of the day. Vow to live it in its total fullness, to honor the miracle of you and your life and this marvelous world we've all been given. Share the day with everyone you come in contact with, live it to its fullest. If there is one more "I love you" left for you to say, make sure it is not wasted. Say it. Say it every night and morning if you want love in return.

Living rich is living full and sharing and loving and enjoying just being. Radio and TV stations sell time as their chief commodity, but once a minute has passed, it can never be sold again. You will have to find out how to optimize each of your moments to their fullest in order to not lose a single dime's worth of life's value. Simply by being aware of the precious time as it passes, you can change your entire life. If you knew how many minutes were left you, what would you do differently? Whatever it is, do it *now!* Why wait and risk having it be too late? Goethe said, "Whatever you dream you can do, begin it. Action has magic, power and glory in it." Fill your life with the magic, power, and glory of taking action toward your goal, of beginning now, today, this minute, to become who and what you have always most desired.

Often we let ourselves get trapped in the roles that others

have chosen for us. We are raised to follow the course that others—our parents, teachers, friends—set us upon. We learn early to adapt ourselves to the routines that are determined for us. To go to school and do our homework and eat our meals and watch TV on someone else's clock. Our clothes are laid out by our mothers, our dinners prepared to her taste. Peer pressure influences our opinions, cultural expectations dictate the course we should find desirable.

It's no wonder, then, that so many of us arrive in our adulthood without a firm grasp of who we are and what we want. It becomes so easy to just continue along the path we were set upon. Complacency requires so little effort.

But a complacent life is not a richly lived one. Complacency does not ignite the sparks of joy and passion and enthusiasm that are needed to succeed. To do that, you need to fulfill *yourself*, to follow the shortest path to your own desires.

How can you know what those desires might be when the mechanism for finding out has been stifled within you? When the muscle of your individuality has atrophied? You can find out by altering your perspective. By shaking yourself up and observing what falls out.

Stand on the dining room table and look at your home. Practice looking from new angles. Take the side opposite your usual one during a friendly debate on some issue. Argue vehemently against the position you have always held. Eat some food you have never eaten before. Wear your hair differently. Experiment with yourself, with your preconceived notions and ideas. Explore yourself. Undertake an art project, draw something or do a collage, write a poem or a story, take up a musical instrument, put on some music and dance!

Dare to be different. Don't be part of the herd. Be yourself. And be more than yourself. Look at life from various perspectives, keeping your outlook fresh and vital. Your life is in your hands, like a piece of clay all ready to be made into the most beautiful expression of art imaginable—the expression of *you*, of your beauty, your uniqueness, your grandeur. You have a singular talent or ability; each of us does. And each of us has a purpose to our lives. Finding that purpose and using our unique talents to accomplish it will bring about the complete fulfillment that we all desire and so richly deserve. Yet the ultimate gratification will come from the journey more than from reaching any particular destination (see Appendix 5).

Explore yourself to find what it is that you were born for. Break free of the chains of expectation and obligation and limited thinking to search out the different perspectives that hold the key to you.

Life is truly a banquet; make sure you taste every course. It is *your* banquet, held in your honor. It is your time to shine and it will be whatever you make of it. It has been said that "you are what you eat"; remember this at the banquet of your life. The result of everything you do will be determined by the courses, choices, and portions you sample as you go.

Seize the day. Grasp it firmly and hold it fast to you. In the final analysis, it is all you have.

Overkill and Inundate

My wife Carole and I were seated at a charity dinner with a newlywed couple, Bob and Marsha. As conversation progressed around the table, someone eventually asked the pair how they had met. They exchanged shy grins, then proceeded to tell us the story.

They'd originally met at a reception following a political debate. They'd chatted about the candidates and the state of politics in general, made some small talk, and then they'd parted.

The next day, Bob got Marsha's phone number from a mutual friend and called her. They went on a date to dinner and the ballet, and though they had a nice time, Marsha confessed she had not been overly impressed. Bob, on the other hand, was quite smitten.

The day after their date, Marsha received a beautiful flower arrangement from Bob. She thought it a very sweet gesture, and when he called later in the day and asked her out again, she accepted.

Bob knew that Marsha did not feel as strongly for him as he did for her; he could tell. But he was convinced she was the woman for him and was determined to win her over.

He sent flowers after every date and then called right away to make the next plans. While they were out, he'd often slip little notes into her purse or coat pocket for her to find later. She admitted they always made her smile and think of him fondly. He was careful to notice things and be helpful—if a bulb was out in a fixture too high for her to reach, he'd wait till she left the room and change it; if the clock on the VCR kept blinking 12:00, he'd set it to the right time while she was otherwise occupied; when her car broke down and he knew she was planning to take the bus to work, he'd show up at the bus stop and give her a ride; during the day when he knew she was at work, he'd call her machine and tell a joke or funny story for her to come home to.

Marsha could not help but be taken by such quiet, sweet thoughtfulness. She found herself looking forward more and more to each new surprise, each new gesture. Then Bob had to go away on a business trip out of the country. Marsha was almost surprised to discover how very much she missed him. His persistence and determination had paid off; he'd won her over completely. When he returned, she asked him to marry her. Joyfully, he agreed.

It was a charming story made even more so by the obvious happiness of the newlyweds. It was also a perfect illustration of a point I have been making to family, employees, and friends for years: If there is something that you want, do whatever it takes to get it. Do not hold back out of fear or shyness or some misguided idea of propriety. Overkill and inundate in pursuit of your dreams.

People today lead busy lives, cluttered with information. Their attention constantly is split in several directions at once. To be heard inside the buzz of all the activity, you must make a "loud" presentation of your offering. Say what you have to say over and over and over again. If they won't listen or can't hear you the first time, come back again. If they've closed their minds, come at their hearts. If they lose you in the rush of life, go after them again.

Don't be afraid of being seen as pushy. If you believe in what you are presenting, nothing should stop you from making others believe in it as well. You will only be seen as pushy or annoying by the people who, for whatever reason, do not want to understand the value of what you offer. And you cannot waste your time worrying about them when there are still plenty of people out there who need what you have and are waiting, even though they don't know it, for you to help them see that. Once you have reached those people, they will not think you pushy, but persistent. And once they realize the benefit you have created for them, they will be glad you didn't give up.

There are people who search for the one "right" approach. They believe there is one magic word or gesture or medium or message that, when they find it, will make people immediately stand up and take eager notice of them. I know business people who have spent fortunes doing market analyses, running focus groups, and assessing demographics, thinking that when the information is all compiled they will have the single best answer to their marketing need.

But humanity is diverse and fragmented. What is right for one person is not right for the next. What appeals to one bores another. What strikes a chord in one means nothing to another. There is no single "right" message or approach that will appeal to everyone out there.

So I spend my marketing money in the marketplace itself, making various different approaches directly to the people. They will determine better than any study or analysis what captures their attention and compels them.

Overkill and inundate. Saturate. Reiterate. Maybe you'll get that first appointment, that initial interview, just because the person you've been pursuing wants to "get rid of you." So what? The point is, you got in. And once in, you have an opportunity you would not have otherwise enjoyed at all. How you got there is irrelevant; just get there.

Life insurance and life insurance salesmen are two things most people avoid like the plague. But I *knew* when I was beginning that what I had to offer was of great value. I knew that what I was selling was badly needed. Most of the people who initially avoided me did so not because of anything I had said or done, but because of their preconceived notions, their unwillingness to address the topic, their fear or discomfort with the concept of death. Or they shied away simply because they thought they already had all the coverage they needed or they had been ill-advised by some so-called expert.

But I knew from the information they had given me during their attempts to get rid of me that they were not adequately covered, that their estates were facing significant tax losses, that their children were going to pay the price of their avoidance. So I persisted. And I persisted. And in over 50 percent of the cases in which I got directly involved with a reluctant prospect, my persistence paid off, both for me and, more important, for them. When I got through the clutter that made up their resistance and showed them the facts of my case, they were, more often than not, astonished and appreciative.

Overkill and inundate. Believe in yourself, believe in your goal, translate your belief into action.

One of the best examples of this philosophy that we see around us all the time is the manner in which politicians conduct their election campaigns. We may roll our eyes in exasperation at politics these days, but since the beginning of democracy those seeking office have practiced saturation exposure of themselves and their platforms. From stumping and whistle-stops, to rallies and paper hanging, to television ad campaigns and debates, candidates use every opportunity to pursue your support in achieving their goal. Whatever you may think of this process or of the individual men and women who employ it, there can be no question that it is effective.

You, as you pursue your goals, are no different from a politician. Whatever your pursuit, you are campaigning, as Bob campaigned for Marsha. You must seek to make people aware of you and what you have to offer in every and any way you can.

In the ads I run in various newspapers and magazines around the country, I reiterate my message, saying the same thing over and over in slightly different ways to capture the interest of different types of people. Were I to pick just one approach, it is conceivable that a person could find a means to discount my knowledge or judgment. But the sum total of my various statements achieves an authority too massive to be dismissed. Each ad builds on the next until they cannot help but be noticed.

Nor do I stop with print ads. I make the same points, present the same messages, in direct mailers and on television commercials and infomercials. I have written three books on the subject as well, and have appeared on TV talk shows. I put myself out there every chance and in every way that I can.

Each forum cross-markets the others. I offer my books in

my print ads, I talk about my seminars on my infomercials. This helps establish a broad, extensive base. I also use a photo of myself in all my materials. It may seem to some people that I do this out of vanity, but I have a much more calculated reason. As a salesperson, half my battle is for personal recognition. What if I were to so effectively promote my product or service that people were clamoring to purchase it, but made no distinction between buying it from me or from someone else? I, and you, need to establish the personal presence, the name recognition, that makes people associate you with your product. Do you need any greater example than Coke®, Kodak®, Jell-o®, Xerox®, or Band-Aid®? These brand names have become synonymous with the product itself. My goal is the same: to make people feel that they want not only what I've got to sell, but to buy it only from me. There are thousands of life insurance salespeople out there. Once I show someone how to use a policy to reduce their estate tax costs by up to 90 percent, there is nothing to stop them from taking my plan to their existing broker and having him execute it. So I inundate the marketplace with me. I establish myself as the authority in this field. Now it's not a plan that people want to buy and are willing to buy from anyone. It's *Barry's* plan, and they come to me.

Whatever you are selling—and believe me, every aspect of every interaction of every goal you set for yourself involves a sale, in one sense or another—your "advertising" must be as thorough and complete and repetitive of your central proposition as you can possibly make it. Don't refine your message, don't narrow your focus. Be broad and expansive and loud and determined.

If you've ever attended one of the Wealth Creation seminars that I conduct each year, you'll know that I begin each one by telling the attendees, "First I'm going to tell you what

I'm going to show you. Then I'm going to show you. Then I'm going to tell you what I've shown you." Some people might find this overbearing. But they can't argue with the fact of my success. Even my detractors can't denigrate my achievements in my industry. They may not like what I am doing, but they have to admit I must be doing something right.

You can use that same basic formula in approaching any goal you are pursuing, any means to living life richly. Tell people what you're going to show them; summarize the point your presentation or approach is going to make. Show them; present all the facts and benefits and be exhaustive in doing so. Tell them what you've shown them; go back and review the information, anticipate questions and answer them, show them exactly how you've proved what you set out to.

It's no accident that this is exactly how our legal system works. At the start of any trial, attorneys for both sides address the jury and tell them what the evidence is going to show and why that evidence is going to support their version of events. Then each side puts on its case, offering the evidence it alluded to in its opening. At the conclusion of the trial, each side again speaks to the jury, summing up how the evidence supported its theory.

You, in your quest for almost any goal, are like the attorney. The person you are approaching is the jury who will determine for or against your case.

People, particularly those who are being sold something, and particularly these days, are inclined toward skepticism. Even though they have chosen to attend my seminar—presumably because they have some need or interest in what I can teach them—they often sit in the audience looking to pick holes in my concepts. They want to be convinced, but they have no intention of making it easy. And that's fine, as long as I or you are willing to do what it takes to be convincing. Overkill and inundate. Overcome their resistance with information and more information, enthusiasm on top of enthusiasm.

Are you looking to advance in your job? Have an idea you'd like the boss to consider? He or she is a busy person and may not fully recognize the value of what you are proposing the first time you present it. Don't give up. Approach again and again. Bring more support, more data. Find the way to make your boss take notice. If you don't, who will? Notice is not conferred upon those who do not seek it.

Are you looking for romance? Follow Bob's lead and, while remaining respectful, do not be swayed from that which you know is right. Can't find your "Marsha"? Make sure your friends and family know you are looking. Run and answer ads. Attend singles functions at your church or social club. Hire a matchmaker. Put up a sign. Do whatever you can think of, saturate and reiterate, remembering that this is the only life you will get and there is no time to waste when it comes to making your dreams happen.

Looking to start your own business? Saturate your self-promotion. Make people listen. Reiterate your value until they cannot help but take notice. If you do not believe in your business enough to promote it, who will?

Remember at all times: No amount of enthusiasm or zealousness is too much or unseemly when the success of your mission is at stake. Overkill and inundate in pursuit of your dreams.

What is your particular goal? Write it down in a simple, declarative statement: "I want to get married," "I want to get my book published," "I want to own my own home," "I want to start my own business." Now think about how badly you want to achieve this goal. Think about how its accomplishment will enrich your life. Then make a list of all the things you could do to make this dream come true. All the steps you can take, all the avenues you can pursue. Do not hold back; write down everything you can think of. Now, being honest, assess how many of those things you're actually doing. If the answer is anything less than everything, you are not doing enough.

Life is fleeting. There is not an infinite time available to you. And you are entitled, as is every person upon this earth, to fulfill your existence in the manner that most satisfies you. Look at your list and think about how empty and futile your life will feel if you do not achieve your goal. Think about how full of regret you will be if you reach your life's end and realize that you failed to do as much as you could have on your own behalf, and therefore did not achieve all that you'd hoped for. These are sad thoughts, but they can also be motivating because they can help you gain a needed perspective. Look again at the list of things you could be doing. Is there anything on there that's so difficult or embarrassing or risky that it is worth denying the fulfillment of your aspirations? Is there anything on there that you want to avoid doing so badly you'd prefer to die without having become who or what you wanted most to be?

Do it all! Take every step. Overkill and inundate, saturate and reiterate. Fear regret more than anything else. Fear futility and a wasted life not richly, boldly lived.

6

Expect Success

Did you ever notice how a beautiful woman who does not know how lovely she is can sometimes come across as plain? She is not noticed, not paid attention to, because she does not feel herself deserving of these things and does not act in a manner that attracts them. Meanwhile, a plain woman who carries herself with the poise and elegance of a great beauty will be responded to as if she is one.

In the same vein, a person who speaks authoritatively on a subject about which he knows absolutely nothing will often garner more interest than a learned man who mumbles and hesitates.

Presentation results in perception. People will tend to believe about you what you believe about yourself. As Eleanor Roosevelt said, "No one can make you feel inferior without your consent."

If you are shy and tentative, behaving as if you doubt the

value of what you have to offer, others will doubt it too. If you have a chip on your shoulder, if you act defensively in anticipation of being put off by people, they will be put off. If you're a "yes man," agreeing with everything people say as if you have no confidence in your own opinion, they will have no belief in you either.

Achieving success requires that you set a goal that is high enough that it provokes your excitement, challenges and entices you. But you also must *believe* that it is possible for that goal to become a reality. Believing it possible will make the desired achievement a reality. And once you've experienced the easy pleasure of succeeding, the confidence and self-assurance that you attain will be implanted so deeply in your mind and spirit that it will become a part of your subconscious. The norm will be the achievement of success and a surpassing of your dreams. Remember, man does not dream beyond his power to achieve.

This positive attitude is the cornerstone for any success pattern. For if you do not believe you can do something, why should anyone else?

The power of suggestion, whether to one's self or to another, is the most important part of communication. How you communicate to yourself is indeed a determining factor in how well you can communicate to others. The message you give yourself that motivates you and stimulates you to enthusiasm will transmit itself to others as an appealing degree of confidence and self-assurance. You must activate your own enthusiasm in order to activate theirs.

Your attitude, then, must be self-assured, self-confident; you must appear to know what you are doing and what you are talking about. These qualities should be apparent at all times, for your attitude is reflected in your voice, your demeanor, your appearance, your body language, your eyes. Attitude is an entirety.

A woman who does some work for me told me a story that illustrates this point perfectly.

The woman worked at an advertising agency as an account executive and was in charge of several accounts, many of which she had developed on her own and brought with her when she had joined the firm. She was good at her job and well liked by her clients. But eventually she came to have some unhappiness with her place of employment and decided to make a change.

Several clients, essentially those whom she had brought in to begin with, opted to make the transition with her. However, one whom she had developed and serviced for several years felt a sense of loyalty to the current agency and decided not to make the move. Nonetheless, the woman and the client remained friendly and kept in touch.

It was not too long before the woman received a phone call from the client, who told her, "We want to talk to you about moving our account."

"I'd be delighted to do business with you again," the woman replied, "but I have to ask, why now?"

The client explained that the firm had lost confidence in the agency. It seems that the woman who had been hired as a replacement account executive made a bad appearance. She dressed poorly, was unkempt, was always late and disorganized in her presentations. Said the client, "I couldn't help but feel that my business was in tenuous hands. I mean, if she couldn't take care of herself, if she couldn't get herself together to dress decently and be clean, if she couldn't take the moment needed to organize herself before coming into my office, how could I have any faith that she could take care of my account?"

The client in that story was reading the signals that the new account executive presented about herself, and was not impressed. The sloppy, haphazard manner of the new account executive did not inspire trust and confidence.

These days there are a lot of people who would read the above story and dismiss it, thinking it to be an example of political incorrectness. They might assume that the client was reacting on a superficial level to the unfortunate account executive's choice of hairstyle or her lack of fashion sense, considerations that supposedly have nothing to do with her professional abilities. Or they might even go so far as to think the female account executive was being discriminated against, judged by her appearance instead of by the standards of accomplishment to which a male counterpart would be held. (Interestingly, the client in this story was a woman.)

But the fact of the matter is, the new account executive was not being judged based on her gender or sense of style, nor on her race, religion, ethnic, or national background. Her individual, professional competence, or lack thereof, was being read in the manner in which she presented itself. And whether we like it or not, we are all judged in the same way, just as we all make similar judgments.

Comportment *does* matter. The sense of yourself that you project matters. If you stride into a meeting confident and secure in your ability, others will see you in the same light. If you expect success, you are much more likely to achieve it. If you act with dignity, integrity, and morality, others will respect you as you respect yourself and them.

With conviction comes attitude. Attitude is an idea, a thought, a persuasion inside your own mind. The self-assurance and confidence that compose your attitude must then produce enthusiasm. And enthusiasm itself is a combination of all the previously mentioned ideas. Persistence is an idea. It embodies an obsession coupled with conviction, which in turn produces enthusiasm. Surely endurance must accompany persistence. If the race requires 200 laps, 196 will not suffice. Four hundred and ninety miles will not bring you to your destination if 500 miles is your journey's length. Too many dreamers with vision and foresight could not, for one reason or another, complete the last lap, go the last mile. I think it likely that, when it came right down to it, they failed to believe strongly enough in their vision. They did not have sufficient faith that they would succeed, and this robbed them of the attitude that would have produced the persistence and enthusiasm to see them through to the end.

An actor auditioning for a role knows that if he stands before the director shy and cautious and stumbling and afraid to assert himself, he will almost certainly not get the part. But if he projects an expectation of success, if he knows he is good and conveys that certainty through his performance, his chances are greatly improved.

An athlete going into competition *must* do so with the conviction of success. Hesitancy is a weakness the competition can exploit; it's a barrier to a smooth, focused, determined performance.

The same is true for you in whatever you pursue. You must expect success in order to achieve it.

Visualize what a successful outcome would entail. See yourself in your mind's eye scoring the touchdown, landing the account, giving a virtuoso performance. At first it may be difficult. You may be distracted by fears of failure; your inner vision may turn to the embarrassing possibilities of defeat. But with practice you can overcome the tendency to negative thinking, which all too many people embrace. Imagine what it would look like to win, learn to see yourself in that picture without reservation or hesitation. Literally close your eyes and create within your mind a film of yourself being the person you have always wanted to be, doing the things you have always wanted to do, accomplishing the things you have always wanted to accomplish. Then practice carrying this vision with you into the theater of your life.

Stand outside the prospect's office for a moment and see the outcome you desire, then go into the meeting holding that image with you. Your bearing, manner, speech patterns, and general conduct will all reflect the serene confidence that potential clients are attracted to and comforted by. You will have already won a major part of the battle.

Place your hand on the phone receiver just before picking it up to call the person you would like to date and feel what it will be like when that person says yes. Then make the call and hear in your own voice the calm, attractive presence that is so appealing to others.

Are you terribly shy or timid? Can't picture yourself succeeding? Try a technique many have used with great success.

Take your middle name and pair it with the name of the street you grew up on or the elementary school you attended to create a new persona, an alter ego, whom you can imbue with the qualities you think you lack. Are you afraid of public speaking and so always speak too quickly or too quietly or trip over your words? Imagine that your brazen alter ego is giving the speech. He can do anything. He is undaunted and unintimidated. Of course, in truth, he is just those parts of yourself that you have difficulty accessing, but it can be very helpful to take those characteristics and invest them in a separate self who takes over those functions you find intimidating. After some time, you will be able to abandon the doppelganger as you gain more confidence from each successful foray into the activity you feared. But the technique can be very helpful in getting you used to expecting success.

Another means of overcoming your fear is to write an account of the successful completion of your task or activity before you have engaged in it. You can frame it as a short story or a letter to a friend, real or imaginary, or a diary entry or conference report. Use any format that feels natural and plausible. If you regularly submit written memos to your boss following new business development meetings, write one prior to a prospect meeting detailing the great success of the encounter. If you keep a log of interview activities, make an entry prior to your next appointment noting the offer you received. If you regularly follow up a contact with a letter reiterating what transpired, write one beforehand that expresses your pleasure at the positive outcome. You may even just jot a simple note of the sort you would leave your spouse, saying only, "I did it!" or "I got it!" or "They were thrilled!"

There is a technique that psychologists suggest to their patients who find it difficult to behave in some desired manner. They tell them to "act as if." Our minds sometimes sabotage our own best interests, making it very difficult to believe in ourselves. Lots of people, from parents to siblings to teachers to friends to bosses and coworkers and competitors, belittle us to aggrandize themselves. Over time we can get worn down to the point where holding good thoughts about our own abilities is quite a challenge. If you find it hard to think of yourself as someone capable of achieving a certain goal, try acting "as if" you were capable. You don't have to believe it, just act as if you did; as you think someone who did believe it would act. You might be amazed at the results. Acting as if you expect success can accomplish the same end as expecting it. And once you accomplish it, expecting it will no longer need to be an act!

The effect of these exercises is to put you into a frame of

mind whereby success is not just possible, it is the probable, anticipated result of your efforts. And this in turn translates into the confidence and presence that engenders success.

There are also physical exercises you can do that might aid you in achieving an ideal state of mind for success. You are an integrated being, not just a mind or a will. Your physical nature affects your emotional state, and vice versa. A crisis in confidence affects more than your behavior, it affects your physical state as well.

When you are calm and confident, your breathing is deep and regular, your pulse strong and steady, your senses sharp and acute. Your body processes more oxygen more effectively and this helps keep your thinking clear and precise. You tend to stand taller, walk with a more relaxed gait, and perspire less.

But when you're tense and fearful, you tend to breathe in a more rapid, shallow manner. You become muddled and slow, clammy and dry-mouthed. Your thought processes are impaired, your reaction time drags. You may shamble along with your shoulders hunched, your hands may tremble, your voice crack.

Just as your emotional state can affect your physical being, so too can your physical state affect your emotional well-being. It works both ways, and you can use that to your advantage.

Before embarking on the course you have set yourself, before stepping through the office door or onto the stage or up to the doorbell, take some deep, controlled breaths. Draw the air slowly into your diaphragm, filling it completely, then continue to inhale until your lungs expand fully. Don't gulp the air, just continue to let it fill you. Hold for a second before slowly letting your breath out. Do this several times and you should notice a change in the way you feel. You should become calmer, more centered, more relaxed. Add a stretch or two to release the tension you hold in your muscles and your stance will become looser and more natural.

I was told once that there is a technique psychologists use when dealing with very upset patients. I haven't verified it, though it sounds logical to me. When a psychologist is faced with someone who is out of control, all worked up and lashing out, he can command the situation by matching his breathing to the agitated levels of his patient and then slowly, consciously, bringing it down. Supposedly, as the psychologist lessens his rate, the patient automatically follows suit. And as the physiological mannerisms calm down, so does the emotional state.

One of the reasons I'm so willing to believe this account is that, to some extent, we've all seen this phenomenon in our everyday lives. When you get in a fight and start yelling, doesn't the other person almost always escalate his or her tension level and vocal intonations to match yours? When you're nervous and jittery, pacing and fidgety, don't those around you tend to become the same way? And, more important, isn't it almost always the one who stays calm in the fight who wins—the one who doesn't get nervous who succeeds where the others fail?

These same principles apply to those who expect success. If you can walk into any situation with your breathing calm and your heart rate steady and your demeanor secure, you will automatically encourage the people around you to feel the same way about you, and probably about themselves when they are with you. What an irresistible combination!

One caution: Know the difference between being confident and being cocky, between appearing secure and appearing egotistical, between expecting to achieve success and demanding others give it to you. The distinctions are hard to pin down on paper. They have to do with the energy you put out, the look in your eye, the way you speak and hold yourself.

Watch the greats and you will learn to see in others the qualities you desire to cultivate in yourself. Michael Jordan expects success, yet he does not have to fiercely declare before each game that he is going to break some record or beat the other team as if he were some federation wrestler. His power rests in the quiet certitude he brings onto the court. Colin Powell exudes the same dignified, low-key confidence. Did anyone doubt that we would win under his leadership?

Visualize, anticipate, expect success and others will expect it of you as well. There is no more powerful weapon in your arsenal of means to a richly lived life.

Be the Best That You Can Be

A nthony Robbins said, "People don't know how to [make the] change," that is, how to change themselves into what they want to be.

Can you make yourself a better player? Can you motivate yourself to achieve your fullest potential? Can you make yourself the person, business professional, family member you would most like to be? Every person, from the president on down, can be motivated to reach a higher level of personal achievement. First you need to raise your standards for yourself. Then you need to know the technique for accomplishing the desired change. Says Robbins, "Success is natural. We have just conditioned ourselves away from that natural success. We have to reprogram ourselves and eliminate all negatives."

Condition yourself so that there is a passion, and this will provide a wonderful life. You must have self-confidence and be willing to pay the price. For most people, the biggest obstacle is fear of failing. Condition yourself for success—see, feel, and experience it, just as Andre Agassi did many times prior to winning at Wimbledon. After his triumph, he said, "It was just the natural thing to do." Since in his mind he had already won the tournament a thousand times, it was a natural transition for him to win it for real. You have to visualize what it is you want. You have to see where you are going.

When you start to walk on your walking machine or begin a two-mile jog around the park, see in your mind's eye the end of that walk or jog; look to the feeling of accomplishment and well-being you will have today and see down the road to the good you will do for yourself cumulatively over time. Perceive it, imagine it, live it, and you will find that your walk or jog becomes easier and more pleasing. Only with the picture of the end result firmly in mind can you successfully and energetically execute the myriad daily drudgeries required by life to move you forward from one moment to the next. If you dream and occupy yourself with where you will be, where you are going, how your efforts will add up to something grand and marvelous, life will become a treat instead of a chore.

Anthony Robbins also told a story about how belief in God is important in everything, but you have to help God; He can't do it Himself. The story involves a beautiful development in the middle of the desert. This piece of land was owned by a man who had bought it twenty years earlier. People remarked how fabulous the land was and how beautifully he had developed it. "God and I are partners," the man would say. "He provided the land and the irrigation to help water it and make it lush. However, I then had to work it.

And for anyone who doubts me, you should have seen what God had done with this land before I became his partner."

Tommy Lasorda, the manager of the Dodgers baseball team, tells how, every time he wanted a cigarette after he'd finally decided to quit, he'd pull a pack out of his pocket and say to himself, "Who is stronger, that pack of cigarettes or me?" And each time, he would reply to himself, "Me." He has never smoked since. Mr. Lasorda apparently applied the same power of will and determination to lose a significant amount of weight. He beat his cigarette habit and weight problem because he *determined* he would do so.

You have the same strength of character. You have the same willpower. All you have to do is believe that you do. Visualize it, express it in the terms that provoke you to feel strong and determined. You can be whoever and however you want to be if you will just take the initiative and responsibility. Don't be swayed from your course by what others are doing; hold fast to your own ideals and your standards. The best defense you have against the chaos of today's quickly changing world is a firmly rooted sense of yourself and who you choose to be.

It is said that there is nothing that changes more than change, and the only thing that is constant is change. Mores, and the perception of these mores, continually evolve to support the myriad of opinions that exist in the world today. What is right for one may not be right for another. But it seems to me that there must be a certain standard of right and wrong that is applicable to everyone in all situations. Without this, civilization breaks down.

Look at the monarchy in Britain, an institution of great longevity, importance, and decorum. The world has careened into such a state that we have a prince of this once-proud house making a mockery of its good name by revealing intimate details of his indiscretions before his queen, his mother, his wife, his children, his nation, and the world. Then, apparently in the name of equality, or feminism, or revenge, his wife, the princess, reveals her own indiscretions to him, her queen, her children, her nation, and the world. What has the world come to that this is totally accepted by many people of various ages, nationalities, and disciplines? While the reactions were diverse, I thought it incredible to see even more people in their seventies and eighties who considered in the name of "change" and the "new world" that this was allowable. What has become of human dignity, privacy, and self-respect that these two supposed royals could so besmirch each other and themselves? There was a report that one columnist, unable to describe a particular outfit the princess had worn because the princess would not identify the designer, remarked, "It is rather incredible that the princess would not reveal the maker of her outfit, but all else is an open book." Rather incredible indeed. Yet there are those who believe that this is proper.

I maintain that we must embrace some sense of basic morality in order to bring the world back to its axis, to re-create the family values and morals that existed during less frenzied times. While the world certainly must change and new concepts be adapted, there must be a basic foundation in one's life that transcends all time and change. It is your job to find that foundation inside yourself and hold firmly to it despite the chaos that rages around you.

Consider, in contrast to the British royals, our own cherished "royal": Jacqueline Kennedy. Mrs. Kennedy always rose to the occasion. Her elegance, charm, and poise brought to every situation a feeling of comfort and grace. She made people feel that she was something special, something that everyone would want to be. And even so, despite the pressures of the myth that surrounded her, in her presence people never felt small. She had the remarkable quality of making everyone near her feel better about themselves and the world they inhabited.

It has been said that it is far better to be associated with a few who are right than with the mob that is wrong, because right is always the winner in the end. But in order to populate the world with more of the people we probably all agree we prefer, we have to become those people. If you want to be surrounded by people who exhibit the qualities of a Jacqueline Kennedy, you must first become one.

Examine your life honestly. No one but you need know the results of your examination, so don't hold back. Which style of morality are you upholding, and how does it support you in your quest for the achievement of your personal best? Can Princess Di be said to be living rich? For all the wealth of Windsor, she seems impoverished to me.

Think of it this way: All of life is a sale. To be the best you can be, you must first sell yourself on your notion of what that means to you, of what it is to be the best you can possibly be. You develop the concept of yourself no differently than you might develop the concept for any product or service. And then you market that concept to yourself and the world around you. Meticulously and with great devotion, Jacqueline Kennedy crafted a notion of the best person she could be. She then embraced that notion wholeheartedly and became that which she envisioned herself to be. In effect, she "bought" the image of propriety, grace, and strength that she had "sold herself" as being the appropriate model upon which to live.

You are no different from Jacqueline Kennedy. You sell yourself all the time. Not in the context of selling out, of diminishing yourself in exchange for some gain. But in the wholly opposite sense of selling to yourself and others the vision you have of yourself. You sell yourself on an idea first, then use your belief and enthusiasm to sell the others whose support you need. You sell a potential new employer on your skills and abilities, you sell a love interest on your qualities and value. Employed properly, this "sales" technique is what will translate your concept of the best you it is possible to be into a reality; the idea into the product.

All of life is a sale in the purest, most noble sense of the word. Every day, you create yourself in the image you choose and then "sell" that image to yourself and the world around you.

What more beautiful thing can there be than the ability to sell? Nothing starts until something is sold—the wheels that turn are powered by sales. The sale is the initiation, the starting point from which everything else flourishes.

When you sell, you are an enigma, an actor, and a technician. You embody the good and bad of any man or woman, you have the ability to bring out the good or bad in every one. Your belief, sincerity, and integrity justify and determine your total approach.

A salesperson comes in many forms. He is the clergy; an attorney standing before a jury; a doctor advising a patient; the president proposing a new plan to address the budget or welfare or defense. He is a child coercing his parents' agreement to some desire, or a baby crying so a bottle is produced.

We are all salespeople, each of us, every day in every way, in every presentation we make to ourselves or to others. We sell ourselves all the time. Salesmanship is, after all, just another form of communication.

If this is the ordinary way of life, if salesmanship is in the everyday scheme of things, can you imagine the end result if that ability to sell is harnessed and utilized to its greatest advantage for the benefit of all concerned? The cultivation of sales ability is the cultivation of your own personality, your approach to life, your philosophies, your attitudes, your relationships to others.

Sell yourself on who you want to be. Then go sell the rest of the world and make them see you as yourself, as you choose to be seen, not as they would cast you in the drama of their own lives. Don't live your life based on someone else's definition of you. Make life accept you on your terms.

Emerson once said, "Nothing can bring you peace but yourself. And furthermore, nothing can bring you success but yourself." Self-confidence, positive mental attitude, and belief is what will make everything begin to happen. Selling yourself on the importance of these things, then selling yourself on the things themselves, will engender a self-confidence that is contagious, compelling, persuasive, and attractive.

In *Wealth 101,* * John Roger and Peter McWilliams say, "Pursue your goal. To live your heart's desire is one of the most loving things you can do. Be grateful; you are already living a heart's desire you had at an earlier time. Enjoy the moment, give yourself a gift of a precious present. You are a walking, talking, living, breathing miracle. Marvel in the miracle of yourself. Astonish yourself. Be awe-full with yourself. Wipe away the cobwebs of the cultural conditioning that tells you you're not good enough, that you're not worthy. You are more than good enough, you are more than worthy, you are incredible and very, very precious."

Take these words to heart. They are beautiful and very, very precious. Use them to remember that inside yourself, you already are the best that you can be. Inside yourself you

*Prelude Press—Santa Monica, CA. 1992.

are perfect. You must simply believe that this is true, visual-ize it, embrace it unashamedly. Sell yourself on the belief, then go out into the world and let your self-assurance sell everyone else. All else will fall into place with surprising ease. Be the best you can be and the best will be yours. Be the best you can be and your life will be rich and blessed.

S T E P

8

Stuff Happens as Life Gets in the Way

*God, grant me the serenity to accept the things I
    cannot change,
The courage to change the things I can,
And the wisdom to know the difference.*

Years ago one of my clients gave me a coin with the nonreligious Serenity Prayer printed on it. I was so impressed with the simple common sense of it that I had more of the coins manufactured and gave them out to people as gifts. Now the Serenity Prayer is cropping up everywhere. A mainstay of twelve-step programs, it is also found on bumper stickers, bookmarks, poster art, and needlepoint patterns. It's in homes, schools, psychologists' offices, new-age shops, trendy restaurants. The only place I haven't seen it so far, and the one I think it may best belong, is in business offices.

What the Serenity Prayer addresses so succinctly is the illusion of control and the notion that life is answerable to our will. Sometimes it is. More often it is not. Accepting and recognizing this truth is a critical part of living rich. It prevents you from futilely spinning your wheels in a situation too muddy to be resolved and lets you get on a more productive path.

Face it: Stuff happens. Stuff which may be beyond your control and relentlessly resistant to the application of your will. Expending energy trying to exert control over that "stuff" is a waste. All you will accomplish is the depletion of energy and time that could have been better channeled elsewhere. And in the process you will aggravate yourself, you will become stressed and tense and depressed, and you will distract your attention from other endeavors that you *could* positively affect.

Earlier I spoke about the need to train and apply your will, to expect success, to cover all the angles in your quest for personal fulfillment. I told you to have a vision and follow it through and not be deflected from your goal by outside forces seeking to thwart or diminish you. I am not now retracting or contradicting any of those prescriptions for a well-lived life. But there will be times when there is simply nothing you can do, when outside forces overwhelm you. It's not shaming, it's simply the reality of being human.

Most people, when faced with a no-win situation, fight harder than ever to best it. Perhaps there is some element of survival instinct that compels us to rage against that which seeks to beat us down. But you have to learn to pick your fights intelligently. To accept that you cannot win them all.

And to not be beaten completely when you lose a single battle. The fact is, most of the skirmishes we find ourselves in are not about life and death. Losing them may cost us some money, maybe even some pride or a dream. But we can earn more money, regain respect, dream new dreams. Railing against the uncontrolled inevitable only keeps us focused backward and trapped in a negative space. To live rich, you must be willing and able to move forward out of defeat toward a new victory.

Not too long ago I developed a new product line for the sale of insurance policies, a way of marketing insurance that demonstrated its true value in a simplified manner never before accomplished. My "Ultimate Gift Certificate" was, in essence, no different from any department store gift certificate or cash gift. Except that it had one important and dramatic difference: It allowed people to greatly optimize the money they had available for that gift by using it to purchase an insurance policy which would provide an increased return upon its redemption. In effect, an available $10,000, saved over years with the intention of helping a child to afford college or get started in life after marriage or provide a little nest egg, could become a $50,000 or $100,000 gift at no additional cost to the giver. That's like buying a $100 Nordstrom gift certificate for $10. Fully backed by the insurer, the "Ultimate Gift Certificate" made the true benefits of life insurance easy to comprehend and even easier to acquire.

It took me months to put the product together and to work out the details of underwriting the program with an insurer. I spent hundreds of thousands of dollars producing the product and its marketing materials, securing Dick Clark as a celebrity endorser, producing commercials and infomercials. I had to overcome a lot of naysayers who didn't feel that what I intended was possible, had to buck a lot of conventional wisdom.

From the moment it was introduced, the product was a huge success. People responded enthusiastically to the presentation and understood the benefit of life insurance in a way they never had before. I had successfully replaced their old negative views about life insurance with a new positive vision of its myriad uses. Things couldn't have been going better.

But, of course, stuff happens.

It just so happened, due to sheer bad luck, that I introduced my new product at a time when the insurance industry was being scrutinized by regulators because a few bad apples had fallen into the barrel. Though they had nothing to do with me, my product, or the insurer underwriting it, others had sparked a controversy that soon extended itself to every corner of the industry.

One by one, concerned insurance commissioners of various states began to withdraw approval for my product. Because it was so revolutionary, the very thing that made it effective, they feared it might be misunderstood. Given the atmosphere at the time, they felt it was too radical an approach even though it had been fully approved and met with all legal guidelines for our industry. The underwriting insurance company tried to bend over backward to accommodate the concerns of the regulatory bodies.

At first I fought the injustice. Not only was I going to have to abandon a successful, expensive project for no better reason than that someone else had been engaging in wrongdoing, but the public was going to lose out on a product it obviously wanted and responded to. I did what I could to work with the insurance company to allay their concerns, but when it became clear that the only way I was going to be able to retain approval to sell the product was by restructuring it in such a way as to remove all real value, I accepted that I had been defeated and the concept was pulled. It was a bitter pill, and I had no choice but to swallow it.

Since then I have embarked on several new projects, including this book. I don't look back, I don't count the dollars lost or the time expended or the effort spent. It wasn't fair, it wasn't right, and if I were so inclined I could rage against the system, beat my head against the wall. But it would get me nothing but a headache.

Two years have passed since I was forced to abandon that project. Interestingly, I just received copies of materials from a different insurance company for a product that is a direct takeoff of the one I launched. In many ways they utilize almost exact replicas of my materials, concepts, and specific promotional wording. They even refer in their materials to "wealth creation," the concept I pioneered in this industry and against which I was so adamantly advised. I could be upset, but that's a legal matter. It *is* very flattering, in a way. And I feel validated to know that the merit of the idea has been recognized. It was only the timing, which I could not control, that was flawed.

One of the things I have learned along my way is that often what keeps us from being able to move beyond defeat is a wrongheaded connection we make between ourselves and the things we do. *I* did not fail, *I* was not defeated. It was not my fault that things happened as they did. I did nothing wrong and did everything right that I could. It was simply that a product of my devising was caught in circumstances too big to be countered.

It's a matter of perspective. If I think of myself as someone who should be able to control everything, if I have my sense of self-worth tied up in that idea, then naturally I will feel personally defeated when something occurs that is beyond my control. And I will be stuck in that defeat. But if I realize that it does not say anything bad about me, does not make me a less effective, less accomplished person to be occasionally bested by "stuff," I can retain my self-respect and my determination and my sense of self-worth, and I can move on.

This way of thinking extends to every aspect of life. In fact, it first came to popularity to help people lessen the stresses and dissatisfactions of their personal lives. To help them live rich.

Look around you at the people you know. Try to discern who among them is happy and content and who is not. I predict that, more often than not, you will find that those who are unhappy are engaged in a struggle against something they cannot control.

I know a fifty-year-old woman who has, to all outward appearances, everything it takes to make life wonderful. She is very attractive, has a loving husband, two good children, one adored grandchild and another on the way. There is money aplenty for travel and indulgence, her social calendar is full, and she does volunteer work that she finds very fulfilling for two charitable foundations.

But for all that, this woman is not happy. She struggles with a sense of failure and low self-esteem, because no matter what she does and how hard she tries, she cannot seem to earn her parents' approval. All her activities, her lifestyle choices, her opinions, even the way she talks and dresses are intended to curry the favor that has for so long been denied.

For close to fifty years this woman has fought a battle she apparently cannot win. She thinks that if she just changes herself, betters herself, becomes something more or different, she will finally earn what has been withheld. And as long as she thinks and feels that way, she will never be happy with herself. She cannot approve of herself and enjoy all that she is and has.

But, in all probability, the approval she so desperately seeks is not hers to earn. There is nothing wrong with her, she is a wonderful, lovely person. Were her parents capable of showing pride or love or acceptance they surely would have done so by now. It is my belief that they simply cannot, for reasons that are their own and have nothing to do with their daughter.

This woman has lost so much time available for the enjoyment of her life and its blessings in seeking something she could not find, in trying to control something beyond her means, in refusing to accept that there are some things we do not have the power to change. Her life, possessing all the elements needed to be a richly lived one, is instead impoverished by the drain on the emotional resources she has sacrificed to an unwinnable cause.

Look at the dissatisfactions in your life, the areas of endeavor that thwart you or aggravate you. Look at the little daily stresses that can get so overblown, the personal relationships—be they with relatives, friends, boss, or client—that are not progressing as you would have them progress. Look at the "bad luck" that comes your way, the "good luck" that doesn't. Assess where you could do something differently to affect the change you desire. But, more important, be honest in assessing where there is nothing you can do. You might be surprised to discover that the latter is more often the case than the former.

Your illusion of control over the people and events in your life may well be adding to your stress and holding you back. There is nothing you can do to change your client or your boss, no way for you to control what "luck" befalls you, no possibility that the world will always order itself in a manner convenient to your needs. It doesn't say anything bad about you that these things are beyond your control, it is simply a fact we must all accept. If you fight against this truth, you will surely lose. But if you embrace it, you free energies previously trapped in its grip to find new solutions and new courses of action.

One of my salespeople once had a client who was driving her mad. He was an older, retired gentleman, cantankerous and contrary. I think he missed the power and importance of running a business and bossing people. He compensated by taking every chance he got to assert his authority over all vendors and representatives.

This man used to infuriate my salesperson. Without fail, he rejected the first several proposals she brought to him. He never gave any reason other than that they weren't "right" or "good enough." He dismissed out of hand the hours and hours of careful work she had devoted to his needs.

In response, the woman worked even harder to bring in proposals that would satisfy him. She meticulously crafted policies that accounted for all the conditions he had set, hoping that this time he would recognize the value of what she presented. Of course, he never did. I doubt he even read or studied or cared about what was in those proposals. He rejected them just to prove that he could.

Finally the woman came to me, exasperated and exhausted. She paced back and forth in my office. "He's impossible," she raged. "I can't win. No matter what I do he's determined to play his games. It's driving me crazy!"

I let her vent her anger and frustration until she eventually calmed down. "Did you hear yourself just now?" I asked. "Were you listening to yourself talk? You said you can't win and he's determined to play his games. So why make yourself crazy fighting? He's the client, he's making the rules. Why not just ride the wave instead of swimming against it?''

"Maybe I should just resign the account," she said dejectedly.

"Why? Don't you understand that this has nothing to do with you? If the client were unhappy with you, he'd have called me by now to say so. He's not exactly shy.

"This is about *him*, his need to feel powerful and in charge, which he does by rejecting your work until he's certain you understand who's boss and will jump to his bidding. Then he'll relent.

"So next time you have a proposal to make for him, let up on yourself, accept the process he will put you through. Don't kill yourself putting together the first several proposals you're going to present when you know he's going to reject them. Hold the best ideas back to present when he's really ready to listen.''

Next time, the saleswoman tried my suggestion and found that it worked. It didn't change anything about the client or the way he behaved or the demands he made or the procedure he went through. But it changed her frustration level. It changed her relationship to this process. She was no longer struggling against it, she was playing into it. As a result, she was happier, calmer, back to loving her work. Back to living each moment of the present more richly instead of being stuck in misery and aggravation.

I often use the image of a fist opening to help people understand the power of this letting-go philosophy. You can try it yourself very easily.

The next time you find yourself agitated and upset, holding on to something that is doing you more harm than good, imagine that your fist is clenched into a tight ball, your nails digging into your palm, your knuckles whitening as you try to keep a grip on a wisp of black smoke. This is, in effect, what you are doing with the source of your stress. You're holding fast to it.

Now imagine opening the fist. It won't be easy; that hand has been clenched so long the fingers will be tense and stiff. But little by little you can relax them, let them uncurl, enjoy the easing of the tension that has held them so tightly, until finally the wisp of smoke escapes and is gone.

If need be, you can actually enact this vision, can clench your fist while thinking about the source of your tension and then relax it and give yourself permission to let the tension go.

One of the best examples I have ever heard for the benefit of letting go of the things you cannot control is also one of the most dramatic and had the potential to be the most tragic. I heard this story secondhand, so I can't vouch for its authenticity, but I fear it is an all-too-common tale these days.

A young man whose health had been declining was diagnosed as being HIV-positive. He was furious at the hand of fate that had dealt him such an unjust blow. He couldn't accept it and expended all his energy in anger and grief and fear. The more he fought against the reality of his situation, the sicker he became. Not only did his denial prevent him from getting the medical help available to him, it was sapping his strength and further depleting his immune system.

Finally, at the desperate urging of concerned friends and family, the young man joined a support group. Already his health had dangerously declined and he could no longer deny what was happening to him.

The group helped him to see that he was wasting his energy trying to control the one thing he could not—the fact of his HIV status—and in so doing he was abdicating control of those things that were within his power, such as his diet, medications, lifestyle, and so on. Once he accepted the bitter truth, he began to regain some of his health. He channeled his energies into fitness and worked with a doctor to alter those aspects of his lifestyle that could be damaging to him. He became as strong in his support of himself as he had been in his denial, and the difference worked miracles.

I heard the story about five years ago from friends who were friends of the parents of this young man. For the writing of this book, I called them and asked how the man was doing. Happily, the answer was that he is doing fine. He is strong and fit and healthy. He maintains the healthful attitude and regimen he adopted when he accepted the fact of his infection, and he currently exhibits no symptoms of AIDS.

Interestingly, though he had no idea of the title of this book when he filled me in on the young man's condition, my friend ended his report by saying, "In all, Barry, we're told he's living a pretty rich life."

Stuff will continue to happen to you throughout your life. What you do with it, how you deal with it, may very well make the difference between living rich and just getting by. Practice telling the difference between what you can control and what you can't. Then apply yourself courageously to make the changes that you can and to accept graciously the things that are not yours to command. If you expend all your energy trying to control the things you can't, you won't have enough left to control the things you can. And in my experience, controlling the things you can is a key element of determining your destiny and choosing the path that best sustains your definition of living rich.

I'm put in mind of the musical *Gypsy*, the story of Gypsy Rose Lee, when Mama sings one of my favorite songs. "I had a dream," she sings, and closes with the memorable lyrics, "Everything's coming up roses." I don't think anything better expresses what I believe to be the proper approach to life. Everything really can come up whatever you want it to be. It is all in your determination, and *you* have the power to make that determination. You *can* control your attitude and the choices you make about how you will perceive and interpret the things that occur in your life. When insurmountable obstacles crop up, you can allow yourself to be beaten by them or you can accept that they happened and move on. When someone does you wrong, you can brood and mope and plot against him, or you can accept what he has done as information into his character. When all is said and done, you are better off for having that information.

It's all up to you. Make the right choice. Choose life, happiness, and peace of mind rather than the turmoil and despair and sense of futility that come from trying to control what can't be controlled and blaming yourself for failing.

There is a story that I heard years ago and have told many times since. A very learned man wanted to know the secret to life. He would ask everyone he met, "What is life?" Unsatisfied with the answers he received from his colleagues, associates, and friends, he sought out professors, psychiatrists, philosophers, and religious men, constantly asking the same question, "What is life?"

Finally the man was advised by the most learned people that he should visit the Dalai Lama in Shangri-La, high in the mountains of Tibet. If he traveled those tens of thousands of miles, if he climbed those great heights, he would find the answer that would put him at peace.

So the man took a ship to the far corner of the earth. Then

he traveled by horse and cart across a great expanse of land until he came to the foot of the Himalaya Mountains. He climbed and climbed and climbed until, exhausted, ragged, and dirty—but hopeful—he reached his destination: a hidden monastery and his audience with the all-knowing Dalai Lama.

"What is it you seek, my son?" the Dalai Lama queried compassionately as the man approached.

"Oh great Dalai Lama, tell me, what is life?"

With all the depth and philosophical insight possible, the great Dalai Lama looked into the man's eyes and pronounced, "Life, my son, is a fountain."

The man, incredulous and puzzled, replied, "Life is a fountain?"

The Dalai Lama, with a quizzical look on his face, answered, "What, it *isn't* a fountain?"

Life is whatever you make of it. Have the confidence to say what you feel and the self-assurance to say it with all that is within you. No singer can hit any note unless he first hears himself hitting it, unless he has complete confidence that the note will be hit. The singer has to see it, hear it, feel it, and only then can he sing it. This is true of any statement you make. This is the secret to accomplishing any endeavor.

Hold fast to *your* vision. Shape your life to *your* will. Seize those moments you can, release those you can't. Control the only real thing you can—your attitude—and you will open every secret to a true, full, and rich life.

S T E P

9

To Thine Own Self Be True—What Price Integrity?

Our world is a complex intertwining of interests and ideas. So many people, each having his or her own agenda, each promoting his or her own goals. In the midst of this, it is easy to be swept away, to lose the firm grounding of your own sense of self and your own knowledge of right and wrong. But to live rich, you must not allow yourself to be carried off on a tide of popular opinion, must not reduce yourself to the following of the path of least resistance. You must "to thine own self be true," must remain resistant to the lure of false and inflated promises, must rise above the simplistic rationales of those who seek only the most instant gratification of the most superficial desires. Personal integrity, applied conscientiously and courageously against the forces that exert pressure upon you to relax your vigilance and accept someone else's biased version of the truth, is imperative to any dream of living rich.

The national budget and federal taxes are big talk these days. During the 1996 presidential race, the topics are on everybody's lips. And as the federal government stalls over budget disputes, the arguments for and against one measure or another are thrown around like so much ticker-tape-parade confetti, designed for dazzle and excitement but lacking any weight or substance.

I listen to financial news a lot. It is, naturally, of great concern to my clients and me. What Congress or the Federal Reserve Bank decides to do with taxes, budgets, interest rates, and the deficit is of critical interest to people planning their estates and using life insurance products and trusts to discount their estate-tax costs. So I listen. And my disgust and my indignation grow.

Mere differences of opinion do not bother me; I understand that different people weigh different aspects of the same equation differently according to their own interests and needs. Particularly when it comes to money, people tend to hear or focus on that part of a situation that will most directly affect them.

Lately, I've seen this most clearly as conversations fly regarding the proposed new flat tax. People seem to latch on to that part of the proposal they think will affect their area of interest most directly. Some people are concerned about the loss of the tax deduction currently allowed for charitable donations. This, they fear, will stop people from giving. But during the Reagan administration years, when taxes were lower—as they would be with a flat tax—people gave more. There is no evidence to suggest that individuals give to charity only for the tax relief they receive. I believe people give because giving is its own reward. And if you reduce people's taxes, they will have more money to use to support their favorite charities.

Other people look at the flat tax and latch on to the proposed cancellation of the current mortgage-interest deduction. But why? Probably because some journalist looking to provoke sensationalism or some politician running in opposition to a candidate proposing the flat tax muddied the waters about the flat tax's effects. People who rely on that mortgage-interest deduction to be able to afford their home are easy targets for a fear campaign. But if they do the math, I believe almost all of them will find that with a flat 17-percent tax that is levied only on their income—not on their investments or capital gains—they will pay less overall, even without the benefit of a mortgage-interest deduction.

A friend of mine, Hal, has a significant amount of money invested in tax-free municipal bonds. His concern is that, under the proposed new system, his bonds won't be tax-free or won't be issued any longer. Where, he wonders, will he put his money to enjoy a tax-free return on his investment? Focused solely on his area of greatest concern and on what will happen to the value of his bonds, Hal neglects to consider that under the proposed system, the capital gains and income derived from stocks and bonds *won't be taxed*, so that effectively all bonds will become like munis. More important, his stocks will increase in value due to lower taxes and greater growth.

In the general debate of the flat tax, the politicians opposing Steve Forbes's plan latched on to the fears of the middle class and aggravated class rivalry by screaming about how the flat tax will benefit the rich by lowering their taxes, which are now at a higher percentage than those of the middle class (and everyone else's). But it is pretty commonly known that the wealthy in America utilize the various allowable shelters and loopholes existing in our tax code to whittle their tax liability down. In many cases, they pay significantly less than the proposed 17 percent. Wouldn't a fairly applied flat tax, levied across the board without deductions and shelter advantages available only to the wealthy, be much more fair to everyone?

Looking at the big picture, the answers seem obvious. But people rarely look at the whole of a thing. They see only that portion they think will affect them, that piece of the pie they want for their own. The fact that accord is not simple or obvious does not trouble me—that people assert their own self-interest first is human nature and, I believe, a part of their quest for a rich life. But I *am* extremely bothered by glaring attempts to win votes by obfuscating an issue or pandering to the common view. Which is exactly what most of the politicians seem to be doing in their campaigns against a flat tax. That has to be the case, because otherwise it makes no sense at all.

One of my pet peeves, and a prime example of governmental idiocy, is the never-ending debate around the issue of taxes and the wealthy. Each time I hear some politician or analyst jumping on the bandwagon and claiming that tax cuts favor the rich—as if this is a bad thing—I want to scream. I am so tired of the half-truths of those public figures for whom the truth is a toy to be manipulated in order to earn votes and higher poll ratings.

Consider this. If I said of a couple about to have their first child that they were embarking on a perilous journey fraught with unimaginable expense and unending responsibility; that their lives were about to be turned upside down and would never be their own again; that they would have to endure the terrible twos and the horrible teens; and that parenthood was a huge burden of obligation, work, sleeplessness, and debt . . . I would be telling the truth. All these things are unquestionably true.

"But, wait!" you're thinking. "That's not the whole story. That's not fair. You've left out the part about the love and the pleasure and the immense delight as the children grow and become people you can be proud of. And then the grandchildren, the pure joy of your legacy. You're not telling the whole story of the mutuality of need and support and how fulfilled your life becomes, how wonderful and amazing the feelings are and how they make all the rest of it worthwhile. You've neglected to include mention of the love that will permeate from that new body and the help that will be there to sustain you in your later years."

Well, I couldn't be accused of lying in my original description. But I certainly didn't tell the truth, either, did I? Because I left out a part, an essential part, that would allow someone to realize the whole truth. And, as far as I am concerned, anything less than the whole truth is no truth at all. An omission, I think, is no different than a lie.

When some politicians talk about the tax issues, they tell less than the truth—no truth at all. Yes, tax breaks *would* help the rich. But that's only half of the story. The truth is —and economic history has proved it time and time again— when the rich do well, it usually benefits the rest of the country. It is the rich who invest in new businesses or expand old ones, putting more people to work which in turn raises more taxes and puts more money into circulation and increases consumer confidence, which increases sales, which puts more money to work, which pays to hire more people, and so on. This is the second half of the truth that many of the politicians are not willing to utter because they fear it is an unpopular truth that the majority of Americans do not want to hear. This may be called trickle-down economics, a term many have come to suspect (due to biased reporting and political maneuvering) of grossly favoring the rich at the expense of the poor and middle classes. But none of the media personalities, analysts, or politicians question our current form of *trickle-away economics*, in which the monies raised by overtaxation are simply wasted and mismanaged. The money that is saved on taxes in a trickle-down economy is used to reinvest, to create jobs, to revitalize the economy in order to bring about unprecedented growth as we enter a new millennium. Surely this is a better plan than the one we have now, which creates nothing but bigger deficits and bigger government and bigger waste. Why do we always try to make the rich poorer when we should concentrate on making the poor richer?

What am I getting at? Why is this diatribe in the middle of my book on living rich? Many reasons. But mostly because I see in this one debate and its many elements and aspects a microcosm of several of this country's biggest problems and a case in point for some of the most important requirements for a richly lived life.

Integral to living rich, I have found, is living *true*. Integrity, honor, self-respect, responsibility, pride. I know that when I feel these things about myself and my business I feel centered, at peace, and in accord with whatever force it is that is larger than myself. All of the people I know who could be credited with having lived rich lives (and who themselves feel that they have) exhibit these same qualities.

And just as so-called trickle-down economics allows money to flow from the rich into the middle-income and lower-income classes, there is a trickle-down function of national morality, I think, that is dripping from the leaders and public personalities of our nation onto the general populace. In ways you may not even realize, you have probably been affected.

It seems that every day we read in the paper or hear on

the news some article bemoaning the decline of our national morality. Crime statistics are up. Domestic violence statistics are up. The number of fathers abandoning their families is up. Everywhere, evidence abounds of this decline and its tragic effect on our national character and welfare.

Where does a nation turn when it finds its moral center being degraded? Where is an answer to this terrible problem that affects us all and diminishes our ability to live rich?

Unfortunately, Americans seem to turn to Congress, hoping someone there will be able to enact legislation that will somehow force people to be better citizens and neighbors and coworkers. In ever-greater numbers, we turn outside ourselves, looking for someone else to take responsibility and someplace else to uphold our principles. But to my way of thinking, turning to government is only likely to make the problem worse.

The only place we can each look for the moral fiber that a society needs in order to live in prosperity and peace is inside ourselves. No matter what other success you may enjoy, you cannot live rich if you are not living true to yourself.

I brought in a new salesman. He came to me from an environment that had been very competitive and ruthless, and he admitted that sometimes corners had been cut in pursuit of the sale. I asked him to become an associate in large part because of the regret in his voice when he told me this. I was sure he was a good man who had simply been affected in a negative fashion by his environment. It is hard to withstand the pressure to do what everyone else is doing, especially when they seem to be prospering from it.

After he'd been with me for several weeks, this salesman came to me after a sales meeting and took me aside. He was very excited. "Barry," he exclaimed, "I just wrote a policy and I'm giving your company its proper percentage allocation of the commissions!" I nodded and grinned, unsure what was so remarkable; this salesman had sold other policies of equal or greater value as the one he'd just closed. Why was he crowing so loudly?

"You don't understand," he went on. "I got this lead from you and then received a referral from that client. While it was *technically* through the company, there is no way you could have known. I could have just kept it." He was beaming. Understanding, I smiled back.

The salesman had discovered that being honest left him feeling better about himself—integral to living rich—than any amount of money he might have cheated the company out of could have.

A great part of our society has become, I am afraid, like the previous office the salesman had worked at: an environment that pushes people into relaxing their grip on the values they know to be right. When our leaders and candidates routinely mangle the truth into something expedient, when our heroes and role models turn out to have feet of clay, when our courts and legal system seem to support the notion that no one is ever really responsible for himself and who he has become, it is no wonder that the country's moral center gets skewed.

If you want to live rich, you have to walk tall and straight within yourself. Your race, color, religion of choice, sexual orientation, gender, age, or nation of origin does not matter. All that matters is that you remain true to who you are and to what you know to be right.

Don't Hear Only the Truth You Want to Hear

Listen with a jaded ear to what you are told and how you are told it. Be courageous enough to hear the whole truth even if it isn't what you want it to be.

Rhonda tells of a friend of hers who fell in love with a man. It was clear to Rhonda and their other mutual friends that this man was not being honest with the woman, was not being forthcoming. He strung her along, sometimes appearing to be very close, at other times backing far away and being distant and noncommittal. But Rhonda's friend *would not* see it. It wasn't that she couldn't. She'd admit the problems or her confusion to her friends. But at any suggestion that the man was not right for her or that she was kidding herself about his intentions, she would get angry and refuse to listen. Because she wanted so very, very much to believe it would all work out, she willfully ignored the truth.

Unfortunately, all this went on for several years. In the end the man finally admitted that he wasn't in love with Rhonda's friend and was not going to marry her. She was devastated. Not only was she still alone, but she'd lost so much time that she felt was irretrievable. Her refusal to look at the truth had cost her dearly.

Don't let your desire or need for something blind you to the truth. Listen courageously; don't sacrifice your self-worth and self-respect in pursuit of a happy lie.

Sometimes it's hard to see or hear the truth from inside a situation. Here's one tip: If people who you know care about you are against something you're thinking of doing, consider very seriously that they may be right. These people may be seeing more clearly than you are, and just because they're saying something you don't want to hear doesn't mean it isn't valid. In fact, the greater your resistance to hearing something, the greater the likelihood that at some level you know it is true.

One of the things I think is most tragic in America today, and probably around the world, is how vigilant you must be in gleaning the truth from the one source you are supposed to be able to trust: the media. Unfortunately, it has become necessary to listen with a jaded ear to most news reporting. The lack of a reliable source of unbiased information is, I believe, greatly responsible for much of our nation's lack of direction and purpose.

We all see the increase in sensationalism and biased reporting in the media. It's around us all the time in screaming headlines and sensational teasers—"Film at eleven!"—and grandstanding on issues. But the magnitude of the problem was brought home to me most dramatically when I recently had the great good fortune to discuss the situation with Pierre Salinger, White House Press Secretary for both Presidents Kennedy and Johnson.

Mr. Salinger had recently authored his book entitled *P.S., My Memoirs*, and was speaking on a cruise I took. After his speech, we spoke at great length on various topics, including the state of the media and its impact on America.

Mr. Salinger told me that my concerns and perceptions were shared by individuals and professionals all over the world. Whereas once you could tell the difference between an item of straight news and an article of editorial opinion, he said, the distinction has become so blurred as to be virtually nonexistent. There is no more straight truth, no more straight reporting. Mr. Salinger went on to quote Bernard Ingham, Press Secretary to Margaret Thatcher. He described four diseases that now afflict journalism:

1. Journalists think their opinions are more important than facts.
2. Journalists think that governments, by and large, do not tell the truth and if they do tell the truth it's not worth writing about.
3. To prove his or her independence, the journalist delib-

erately takes a stance against a government, because only someone who is against a government can establish his or her credibility.

4. Journalists concentrate more on the prurient human-interest aspect of stories than on providing unbiased news.

How can the citizens of our country, or any country, be expected to live true to themselves when they are not given the unbiased truth in the information they rely on? No wonder the nation is declining. But you must rise above the temptation to accept the easy version. You must resist the urge to believe what is convenient or popular. Question and doubt. Listen with a jaded ear.

It is remarkable how a population can rise collectively beyond individual interests to really understand true facts when they are given them. However, as long as we are fed distorted material representing a party view or a sensationalized attempt to gain ratings or sell more papers, the overall integrity is lost and the cohesiveness falls apart.

Pierre Salinger confided in me that he and many others see this as a major problem. In fact, he informed me that at a recent international meeting of journalists, press secretaries, publishers, and interested citizens to discuss the deterioration of news reporting around the world, four resolutions were passed in the hopes of beginning to address the problem. While there is no evidence that these resolutions are being utilized or implemented by the media, they at least give you an example of what is so important in a country being "true to itself" whether it is at the national, state, city, or individual level. The resolutions were:

1. On the government side, we must see a rise of open-

ness to the media and we must also see less hiding and manipulating information.

2. On the media side, we must see more honest coverage of important events that affect democratic populations and the future of their countries.

3. Both worldwide government spokespersons and international journalists must raise their ethical standards so that the people's trust in government and journalism can improve from the current low level.

4. Democracy is in part based on the free circulation of information and on the right of citizens to be informed on all matters of general interest. This imposes an obligation on both journalists and press officers in the service of public powers to cooperate and provide citizens with a continuous flow of truthful information.

By the way, did you ever hear anything about this conference and its conclusions reported on the news?

Consider these resolutions as they pertain to your own integrity. Then listen carefully to how those around you present important issues. Consider the source before incorporating the information into your world-view, so you can avoid unwittingly corrupting your sense of justice and truth.

Consider the Source

Remain critical of what other people may have to gain from what they are saying or doing. Be aware of hidden agendas and take into consideration whether there is a possible ulterior motive someone might have in convincing you to support a particular point of view.

Be wary of politicians, activists, or salespeople who have an obvious stake in getting you to support their proposition.

And be careful of others in your life who may want things of you or from you. This is not to say that you shouldn't trust people. But you should keep your eyes open as to what effect the people around you and the situations you're in are having on your life. If you're happy and feeling fulfilled, don't look to change anything. Why would you? But if, like many people, you feel that you're not getting what you need or want or expected from your life, that somehow you've let yourself down, given something precious up, then you should question the things you have blindly embraced in the past. Consider that you may not have been truthful with yourself about what and who and how you are.

The salesman I spoke about earlier, the one who came from the environment where everybody cut corners, said that when he asked one of his coworkers if something he was doing was wrong, he was told it was fine and not to be bothered by it. Everyone did it; in fact, it was expected. "I believed them," he told me, "because I wanted to. But when I thought about it I realized he had to tell me that because he was doing the exact same thing. He needed to dismiss the wrongdoing I was engaging in order to salvage his own conscience. I just never considered that he'd have a motive to mislead me, because I never wanted to think about it either."

I asked if he did anything differently since he came to this realization. "Yes!" he exclaimed. "Now, if something I am told doesn't feel right—you know what I mean, if it just feels off—I don't bury the thought in the back of my mind to avoid having to pursue it. I immediately start listening to the alarm bells. And I question right away if the person I'm dealing with might have a reason to try and cut corners on me. What they might gain. Then I work from the truth, and even if it's harder or takes longer or doesn't yield the same immediate gratification, I go home feeling good about myself."

Stand Up for What You Know Is Right

It's not enough that you find the truth; you also have to be willing to stand against those who have not. It's hard to do, to take the high road and resist the pressure to accept what everyone else is accepting. But you can't go home at the end of a day and feel good about yourself—surely the very first step toward living rich—if you've stayed quiet in the face of wrongdoing. I have enough faith in the basic character of humanity that I still believe that, with the exception of some truly mentally unsound people, we all have consciences and a sense of right and wrong. I believe that we all suffer a loss of self-respect and a feeling of shame that can eat away at happiness and peace when we don't do the right thing.

I'm thinking, as I sit here with Rhonda writing this, about the musical *Les Misérables*, one of my favorites. There is a scene in it that particularly emphasizes this point. Inspector Javert, a police officer who has chased Jean Valjean for years, finds a man he thinks is Valjean and is about to arrest him and send him to prison. Valjean sees the whole thing and thinks what good fortune this could be. If Javert is satisfied that he has captured Valjean, he will stop chasing the real Valjean. But even as he considers this, Valjean knows he cannot do it.

He questions himself about how he will be able to face his fellow men or how he will ever face himself again, and he steps forward to face whatever must be faced. It is, I think, one of the most triumphant and stirring moments in a very triumphant and stirring musical precisely because it ignites in us the desire for that sort of brave self-possession, for the upholding of what we know inside us to be right.

Stand up for your truths. Step forward and claim yourself and what you think to be right. If you hang back and let others dictate a code of behavior that is at odds with your own, you will be doing yourself a grave injustice. Speak out.

If everyone around the water cooler is willing to accept at face value that tax increases for the rich are better for the country and you think they are not, say so. If you don't say anything, your silence implies that you agree. You will have swallowed back an important part of yourself. And the more we get accustomed to swallowing those parts back, the harder it is to recover ourselves individually and as a community.

"I'm mad as hell and I'm not going to take it anymore," shouted the commentator in the film *Network*. Living rich means making yourself heard, standing up for what you believe in. It's your country and it's time you were counted. You can make a difference!

Forgive Yourself

I hate the phrase, "I'm only human." It sounds to me like a denigration of all that is wonderful and miraculous about each and every one of us. There is no such thing as being "only" human. And yet we each possess certain frailties and imperfections because of our humanity. These do not diminish us individually or as a group; it is simply a fact of our existence. There is nothing wrong with possessing these imperfections. The only problem comes about when people try to deny them.

Face up to and understand your frailties and forgive your errors. Realize that you cannot be perfect in an imperfect world. Admit your wrongdoings, first to yourself and then to others. Declare for all to hear, "I have erred. I did wrong. I can do better. I will do better, but I take full responsibility for what I have done."

History shows us the wisdom of this course. Consider the case of President John F. Kennedy. His worst mistake was the Bay of Pigs incident. But within two weeks after this disaster, he took to the airwaves and presented the mistake he had made to the media, his constituents, the American public. By revealing and admitting his error, he revealed his humanity and sparked an even better camaraderie with the American public. He gave people permission to err—after all, how hard must I be on myself if even my leaders can make mistakes and admit to them?—and this endeared him to us. It also demonstrated a type of integrity and honesty that was reassuring.

The end result of the Bay of Pigs disaster and President Kennedy's revelations was that his approval rating went up in the polls to a higher level than it had ever been before. People want you to be right, but they will understand if you are wrong. What's more, they will have compassion since they have been there too.

Remember, "To err is human, to forgive, divine." Forgive yourself and let others forgive you, and you will have mastered a crucial obstacle on the course to living rich.

Take Responsibility

I read a newspaper item about a court case that I found so outrageous I couldn't stand it.

It seems a couple of workers at a factory went to find out why a certain piece of equipment was not working. When they got to the right spot, they found the opening into the piece of equipment was surrounded by stanchions and a chain. A big sign was posted that read, "Stay Off. Danger." They climbed up onto the piece of equipment, brushed past the sign, and stepped over the chain. The hatch into the engine was locked, so they pried it off using one of the stanchions to hammer at it. Finally they got the hatch open and were looking inside when one of them slipped, fell inside the hatch, and wound up mangling his leg to such an extent that it had to be amputated.

He sued.

And won.

Several million dollars.

He claimed the manufacturer was at fault for making the hatch big enough for a person to fit through, and his employer was at fault for, get this, not providing adequate supervision to keep him from wandering off!

And he won.

Several million dollars.

More and more, it seems, our courts, schools, and workplaces are being buckled by the weight of people who have abdicated all responsibility for their own lives and choices. These two men had to run a gauntlet of obstacles to get to a point where one of them could get hurt. They had to willfully and with great endeavor *work* at getting hurt, and then they claimed it was someone else's fault.

Everything is used as an excuse—but not by the person who wants to live rich. That person knows that taking responsibility for him- or herself is far more rewarding than any judgment a jury could hand down.

There are things in all of our pasts that were less than optimum, maybe far less. But as adults there comes a time when we have to stop blaming our parents or friends or society for what we have become and simply decide to become who we want to be. Whatever injustice has been perpetrated against you, it is not so great as the injustice you perpetrate against yourself when you abdicate responsibility for your life and waste yourself blaming yesterday for what you do not have today, instead of doing what it will take to get it for yourself tomorrow.

In *Hamlet*, Polonius advises his son, Laertes, as Laertes is getting ready to sail away, "This above all: to thine own self be true, And it must follow, as the night the day, Thou canst not then be false to any man."

I cannot help but wistfully imagine what our country would be like if everyone upheld that simple principle: To thine own self be true. If everyone told the truth and didn't promote his own agenda at the cost of truth. If everyone took responsibility for his own truth and stood up to be counted.

Neither you nor I can do much to fix the ills of the country or the world as a whole. All we can do is whatever it takes to make life rich and rewarding for everyone. This would make for a better world. And this is best accomplished by being true to ourselves.

STEP
10

Know When No
Means Maybe

I know what you're thinking. You're thinking about Antioch University's rules of conduct, about sexual harassment and political correctness. "If we've learned anything," you're thinking, "it's that *no* always means *no!*"

You're right, of course. No means no. Period. There is no simpler, more important lesson that applies unilaterally across the board. No means no and is to be respected unequivocally and completely.

But that doesn't mean that the next time you ask they might not say yes.

Think of it this way. Peter asks Jane for a date. Jane says no. Peter must respect Jane's no. There is nothing he can do about it at the time, but he can ask again some other time. And it's possible he may have better success the next time. Maybe the man Jane was dating before is no longer in the picture and she's now available. Maybe Peter's persistence makes her look at him in a new light.

Another example. Mary asks her boss for a raise. He says no. That's it, Mary, no raise—right now. But a month from now, Mary might ask again and get it. Perhaps by then the company's financial picture will have improved and her contributions can be better rewarded. Perhaps some project she was working on will have netted big results.

If these examples seem a bit facetious in light of the huge social ills that are being perpetrated all around us because people do not respect that no means no, I apologize. Certainly it is not my intention to be flippant or insensitive. But my point is a valid and important one.

People say no for all sorts of reasons. Sometimes those reasons have nothing to do with you or what you are asking for. Pushing yourself forward at that time is inappropriate and disrespectful and wrong. But asking again some other time may get you the result you desired. The trick is knowing when to ask again. Unfortunately, I'm not sure I can tell you exactly how to know. A lot of it is just instinct.

But I believe you can develop that instinct through trial and error. It's like the muscle memory that enables your body to learn to do something—lift weights, or ride a bicycle, or master a dance routine—so instinctively that your mind seems uninvolved. You practice the activity, paying conscious attention to how things feel and what is happening, until eventually it becomes second nature. The same technique applies here.

Pay close attention to inflection and body language when talking to people. Watch the differences in stance and volume of voice and speech patterns between when they are being receptive to what you are saying and when they are not. I have found that people generally speak in shorter, more clipped sentences when they have already determined to turn me down and in longer, more complex sentences when they are open to what I'm saying. Somewhere in the middle is the "maybe" zone. When they intersperse abrupt, clipped speech with a relaxed, more rambling style, I know they have mixed feelings. So if the outcome of that conversation is negative, I know there is an opening for me to come back.

Some people display their ambivalence directly through their body language. If sitting back with arms folded tightly across the chest is the posture of someone who is closed and defensive, and leaning forward into the conversation is the manner of someone open and eager, then people who lean in and then push back are floating in between. Usually the undecided will say no because it feels safer and does not require an investment they are not entirely sure about—whether that investment is financial, emotional, or time-intensive makes no difference. It is important that you realize that an opening may still exist if you are going to work toward what you want in your journey to a richly lived life.

I had a client many years ago who had some old policies in his portfolio that were no longer appropriate to his circumstances and needs. He kept coming to me for new policies as his finances changed and I kept telling him he needed to let me convert those old policies into something that would work much better and make more sense. But he kept saying no. I couldn't imagine why. He had nothing to lose and quite a bit to gain and I hated to see him wasting money on a product that would not adequately serve his needs.

Something told me that when I finally understood this man's true objection, I would have the means to overcome it. So every couple of times we talked, I would bring up the old policies. I would explain, from different angles, why they were inappropriate and how we could improve them, hoping

I might touch on the one thing that would finally make him see the light. He continued to resist even when I'd countered all of his objections, though he never said in any unequivocal manner that he didn't want to talk about it anymore.

One day this client and I were talking and I again brought up the old policies. "Tom," I said, "I still don't understand why you won't let me save you money and get you better coverage by converting those old policies."

"Oh! Yes," he said, "I'm glad you mentioned that. I wanted to talk to you about it and would have forgotten if you hadn't said something."

I was flabbergasted. Suddenly he was completely amenable.

"I have to ask, Tom: Why now? After all this time, what's made you finally see the light?"

Tom explained to me that he had bought those old policies from his brother-in-law, Stanley, before Stanley had retired and Tom had started doing business with me. He'd understood that what I was saying made sense, but he felt it would be disloyal and a slap in the face to Stanley to change the policies. Now, after a long illness, Stanley had passed away. While Tom felt bad about that, he also felt free to make the changes without hurting his brother-in-law.

Tom's repeated refusals of my proposals had nothing to do with me or what I was telling him. He'd understood and agreed with my position all along. But he was too loyal a man to risk hurting an aged and ailing brother-in-law, and too dignified a gentleman to tell me the true reason for his resistance.

So what I'd seen in Tom's posture and manner and willingness to keep having the same conversation was his being torn between what he felt he should do and what he wanted to do. If I hadn't persisted, if I'd let the matter go the first or second or even third time that Tom put me off, in all likelihood he would never have changed those archaic policies for something much better suited to his need.

Many people are intimidated by the answer no. They feel personally rebuffed and chastised for having asked, and they fear they will offend by ever asking again. They are so attuned to their own insecurities and vulnerability that they cannot focus their attention to correctly ascertain what is transpiring. Had my feelings been hurt by Tom's apparent unwillingness to listen to me, had my ire been roused when he wouldn't believe that I knew what I was talking about, I probably wouldn't have persisted in my course and would never have gotten to that day when he finally said yes.

A young woman of my acquaintance wanted to be an actress. She participated in all her high school drama department productions, acted in summer stock, took voice and movement lessons. When it came time for her to go to college, she wanted to major in theater. The school she selected had an audition requirement for students majoring in acting. This woman prepared her materials, drove the three hours to the school, and performed her audition. She was crushed when they rejected her.

"At first," she told me, "I was so hurt and embarrassed. I felt that, if I was so bad they didn't accept me, I must have made a fool of myself by even trying. I about gave up on the dream altogether. I wouldn't consider any other alternatives, wouldn't go audition at any other schools. I took their no as a reflection of me personally, of my talent and ability. Like it wasn't just my audition they rejected, it was *me*, all of me. It never occurred to me to consider that maybe I'd just had an off day, or maybe they had. Or maybe I'd let myself be overwhelmed. I just took that no as the final word on my dream.

"When my mother pointed out that the school entrance

materials stated that if the first audition was rejected a student could petition for a second chance, I thought she was nuts. Who in their right mind would go through such humiliation a second time?

"Well, my mother made some pointed comments about the flimsiness of my dream and how it was good that I'd gotten rejected now because I obviously didn't have what it would take to survive long in the brutal entertainment world. Her comments stung . . . a lot. But when I got over being hurt and mad, I realized she was right.

"I petitioned for a second chance and argued persuasively why they should grant it, and they did. I made major changes in my audition material, asked one of my old directors for help, and I passed the second audition and got accepted to the school.

"I didn't stay with acting for long," she concluded, "but the lesson I learned has stayed with me. I no longer take no personally; I just come back to things later, or from a different angle, or with new focus, and ask again. It doesn't always work, but often it does. Certainly more often than if I never tried."

Listen very carefully when someone tells you no. As soon as possible after the conversation has occurred write down, as close to verbatim as you can, *exactly* what he said and what the reasons were for the rejection. Stay focused on the task at hand and try not to let your personal feelings get in the way.

Now let some time go by. A few days, a week. During that period you will probably brood about the refusal, particularly if it was something you wanted very much. You will have a broad spectrum of feelings that may range from anger to sorrow to hurt to grief over having lost something intangibly important to you. Rejection can provoke all of these feelings and more.

It's also likely that during that time the no you heard will loom large and unchangeable in your mind. It may seem carved in stone, monolithic.

But these feelings will subside as life's routines turn your attention elsewhere. When some time has passed, look again at your written record of the conversation and the stated reasons for the refusal. In many cases, maybe even in most cases, you will find that what you wrote has none of the dire overtones you thought you remembered. Your mind, filtering what you heard through the layers of your own insecurities, had added colors to the conversation that may not have really been there in an objective sense. Now you can proceed with a rational evaluation of the circumstances to determine if a second try is in order.

You can use your written log to determine the specific points that led to the refusal in order to answer them. You can glean a sense of the mood of the person you were talking to and what else might have been happening in his or her life to provoke a negative reaction to you. Distance will let you gain perspective, and perspective will let you see more angles more clearly.

You might be surprised by what you discover when you look at situations in this light.

Another salesperson who worked for me kept getting put off by a prospect. The potential client had read my book *Die Rich*, and called us for a proposal. Yet, though the salesman had prepared several different methods for her, the client kept rejecting them, giving reasons that made no sense or giving no reason at all other than, "It's not what I'm looking for."

My salesman was completely frustrated and came to me

suggesting that I assign someone else to the case. "I think she just doesn't like me," he said in frustration. "I can't figure out any other reason for her constant rejection of the plans I propose."

I pointed out that if the client hadn't liked him personally she probably wouldn't keep taking his calls and might have even called me directly to request a reassignment of her case.

He said he hadn't thought of that, and his agitation was somewhat soothed—none of us enjoys feeling disliked—but his confusion continued.

Finally he was at his wit's end. He was talking to the client, explaining yet another method for accomplishing her goals (which he had prepared along the stated guidelines of her last refusal), when she rejected his plan yet again.

"Mrs. Smith," he blurted in his exasperation, "I don't understand what's going on here. You reject everything I propose, yet you keep coming back. You say no, but I think I sense from your tone and manner that you want to say yes. I'm afraid you simply don't like me and are making a point of refusing my suggestions as a result. If that is the case, please simply say so and I will get someone else to help you."

He was astonished to hear her reply. In an embarrassed and shy manner, the client finally confessed what her reluctance was about. She told the salesman that contrary to disliking him, she actually liked him quite a bit. She found him bright and charming and diligent and polite. She hadn't been aware of what she was doing, she said, but she was obviously prolonging the sales process to continue to have a reason to talk to him. Not until he stated his observations about her behavior had she realized what she was doing. She was very grateful that he hadn't just given up on her in light of what must have seemed to be very garrulous behavior.

What I saw that my salesman—in his emotional state—

did not, was that the client's behavior was very different from what she was saying. This is a good clue to the likelihood of no meaning maybe—a clue I learned through dozens of similar experiences over the years. Though she kept rejecting him out of hand, she kept coming back and responding positively to his approaches. When the behavior and words are at odds with each other, it is likely that the person you are talking to is not as fixed in his or her position as it may seem.

So watch people. Listen as much to *how* they say things as to *what* they say. Set aside your own emotional responses to rejection long enough to objectively evaluate the situation, and observe how behavior gives clues to real intent. Learn to know when no means maybe. Mastering this awareness is a wonderful negotiating technique, a marvelous way of preventing your dreams from falling victim to someone else's bad day. Don't let a simple, single rejection of your request become a rejection of you and your right to live rich.

Create Reactions

We've all heard the same story, or some variation upon it. It's usually set at a trendy Los Angeles restaurant, one frequented by entertainment-industry movers and shakers. There's a commotion and a young woman rises from her table yelling at the young man who is apparently her date. She is quite furious as she screams at him for some infidelity he's committed. The fight escalates until she suddenly slaps her date across the face, a ringing, stinging slap that can be heard throughout the dining room. A major scene ensues, and depending on the version of the story being told, it progresses into a tantrum, a food fight, an injury, someone fainting or choking or being asked to leave and then fighting with the restaurant management. But it generally ends the same way.

With a single word to her boyfriend, the woman stops the fight. All is as if it never happened except for the mess, the quiet, and the shocked faces of the other patrons. With a quick readjustment to her skirt and blouse, and a nonchalant brushing away of her bedraggled hair from her face, the young woman musters her dignity, turns, and walks over to one of the nearby tables and addresses the men sitting at it.

"Before you say a word," one of the men says, "I recognized the 'fight' from the script."

"I couldn't even get in to audition," the young woman offers by way of explanation.

"You can now," the man responds. "It was a completely outrageous thing to do and I'm hesitant to reward it, but I have to admit, you were good."

I don't know if this story, or any of its multitude of variations, is true. But I know it's believable, which is the truly important part. We recognize that the story could happen, that the actress's method of getting attention is plausible. This is important because it illustrates the common acceptance we have of a lifestyle philosophy we may not be consciously aware of.

What works for the young lady in the story is that she knew how to create a reaction and wasn't afraid to do so. In this way, she fulfilled her immediate goal to get an audition for that part.

To be memorable, to stand out from the crowd, you have to provoke a response in people. Create a reaction and half your battle is won.

Watch a group of adults interacting with a group of children, maybe at a park or a company picnic or the local swimming pool. Who is the one the kids gravitate to? The one who sets aside propriety and inhibition to behave in a manner that grabs the children's attention. This grown-up is creating a reaction from the children, is relating to them in a way that amuses them. He or she is developing the rapport that will lead to a rich family life, a mutual sharing and bonding that begins by provoking a response.

Think about the many ways this attitude is applied. When you read to your children, do you dryly recite the words in a boring monotone? If so, your children will surely be bored as well. But, if you play the parts, changing your voice and your volume and your facial expression, you will draw your child into the story and lay the foundation both for a delightful interaction between the two of you and for a love of stories and books that will stand your child in good stead for all of his or her life.

When you go to a party at which you know no one but the people you came with, how do you make new friends? Hanging back and being reserved won't do it. Few people will take the time to seek out a new person and initiate conversation. No, you have to create a reaction. Join in the conversation, tell a joke, participate in a game, even bring along an unusual food item that provokes attention and breaks the ice. There are something like 5.7 billion people on earth, according to the *1996 World Almanac and Book of Facts*.* If you want to be one who is remembered, you have to make a special impression.

Let's say you happen to meet someone to whom you are attracted at that party (or anywhere, for that matter). How will you get that person to notice you? Think about Bob and Marsha, the couple I spoke about earlier. Bob created a reaction in Marsha with his thoughtfulness and perseverance. You can do the same to the person in whom you are interested in a myriad of ways.

Your methods need not be extravagant or flashy. Even something as simple as making direct eye contact or winking

*Funk & Wagnalls—Mahwah, NY. 1996.

can provoke attention. In fact, just being nice can be an uncommonly thoughtful act. But one thing is certain: You will never get what you want by waiting for it to happen to you. Create reactions in the people who are able to help you further your goal, or who are the object of your goal, and your chances for success increase greatly. This is a vital key to living rich.

People who come to my seminars or see my television infomercials sometimes say that I am overwhelming. But would you like to know how many of them become clients? "If you're willing to say it *that* strongly," one such client quipped, "it must be true." I get noticed in stores and restaurants, my name is known throughout my industry and all over America as a result of my print advertising and TV commercials. All of which aids me in making new contacts, and all of which stems from my ability to create memorable reactions in the people who see or hear me deliver my message.

They say in the entertainment industry that "there is no such thing as bad publicity." In other words, any attention your draw to yourself, be it positive or negative, furthers your purpose.

I don't think this is true. Some types of negative publicity, especially in our newly sensitive, politically correct society, can be quite detrimental. There are certain kinds of attention you definitely would not want to call upon yourself. For example, although dancing at the party hypothesized above with a lampshade on your head would definitely create a reaction, it would almost certainly not engender the type of reaction you desire. However, I do believe that any sort of notice is better than none at all. You might have a chance to salvage disastrous publicity, might be able to use the spotlight created to illuminate your good qualities. Conversely, if you're lost in the shadows, you're simply lost. And since none of us lives in a vacuum, I can think of no situation in which being lost in the shadows would be advantageous.

Of course, one of the most useful applications of this philosophy occurs in the business forum.

Business people in every industry must compete among themselves for new clients, new contracts, new financing dollars. Making proposals and approaches is an everyday aspect of life, and an aspect upon which the success or failure of a venture can depend.

Creating a reaction in the people you are soliciting is of paramount importance. If the would-be client is entertaining proposals from several firms, you must make a memorable impression or lose out.

Perhaps that impression can be made simply by the strength of your proposal or the depth of your experience or the attractiveness of your terms. But generally speaking, no matter how strong all of these factors may be, the final decision will still hinge on how well *you* impress the prospect, how much of a positive reaction you create.

A woman who does some work for me found a wonderful approach. It seems that in her industry, each year at Christmastime a tacit, covert competition takes place to select and present clients with the most imaginative and expensive gifts. Over the years the competition has become so heated that clients are now receiving crystal decanters with forty-year-old bottles of scotch, designer pen and pencil sets, personally engraved gold money clips, and much more.

This woman could not afford to compete at this level for her clients' approval. And, she told me, she found the whole thing rather offensive and distasteful. So instead she spent several evenings and both days one weekend baking cookies. She made over 120 dozen cookies of ten different varieties.

And they were wonderful! (I know because I was a lucky recipient of one of her baskets.)

She arranged the cookies in aluminum foil roasting pans that she decorated with magazine photos, stars, and other holiday embellishments. She then sealed them in plastic wrap tied with festive curling ribbon and took them to her clients. The whole production cost her less for all her clients and prospects than her competition was spending on each gift. Yet the time and energy and thoughtfulness that went into her gift were recognized and greatly appreciated. Furthermore, this shrewd woman made up several baskets for the larger firms she did business with so that not only the bosses received goodies. She also made sure to take a platter to the accounting department and secretarial staffs who, she knew, were more responsible for the smooth day-to-day management of the account and who were often overlooked by other contractors.

In her simple, heartfelt manner, this woman made a greater impression and created a more favorable reaction than all her big-spending competition combined.

Another story, which an associate of mine told me during a conversation about this chapter, illustrates the same point.

The sales and marketing council of a major local industry was having its annual awards program. The council's board of directors had selected "Carnivale" as the program's theme. Now, as was customary, the various advertising agencies affiliated with the industry would vie for the privilege of chairing the event, a very visible contribution with a lot of opportunity for favorable notice.

To secure the position, all the agencies make presentations to the board, detailing how they will bring the theme to life in terms of entertainment, decor, host, and graphics. The presentations are made in person with written copies submitted for later review. After all the presentations are made, the board votes and announces its decision.

The presentations follow one another throughout the afternoon of one day. For the board members, it can be tedious and overwhelming. Knowing this, one intrepid presenter undertook to create a reaction in as memorably uplifting a fashion as possible.

This usually staid, respectable young man arrived at the offices of the board's president in full calypso-type costume. He brought a boom box with him that filled the room with Carnivale music he'd found at the library, and he even brought along some appropriate props. His written proposals were decorated with computer-generated icons of stylized suns and people doing the limbo and steel drummers and costumed revelers. They were printed on bright, colorful paper.

Of course, had his proposal been weak, these gimmicks would not have deflected the board's attention from that fact. But in addition to the considered, thorough job his agency had done, his presentation was an infectious demonstration of his enthusiasm and creativity. His agency won the competition.

I like these two examples for many reasons. They both clearly show how putting some of yourself out there to create a reaction can make a difference in developing or sustaining a relationship (business or otherwise). In addition, in both cases it was creativity and ingenuity, not money, that generated the favorable response. You do not need to be rich or extravagant to make an impression, though it may seem so in today's world. Putting heart and spirit into your approach will earn you far more regard than you could ever buy.

Think about the ways you might do a better job of creating reactions from the people and situations in your life. The number of ways is virtually infinite. I have interviewed people who have submitted resumes to me that are created to look like an insurance proposal. They demonstrate the person's familiarity with our field in a tangible and entertaining fashion. I know a woman who had a quote appropriate to her personal business philosophy printed out on the computer and affixed to the outside of her briefcase. I look forward each time she visits to reading what new quote she has; they are always thought-provoking and interesting, and this simple method reveals a great deal about her ideas and ideals. One gentleman with whom I do business has a new joke each time I talk to him. Even when the conversation will be about routine matters, I look forward to it.

The woman did not write her quotes, the man did not invent his jokes, neither spent any money. Yet each, in his or her own simple, understated way, has made a tremendous impression on me. You can do the same.

For practice, make a list of the people who have made the greatest impressions on you. Is there a teacher from grade school who stands out in your memory from all the rest? A babysitter? A counselor at camp? Someone with whom you work, or a member of your social circle, who always seems at the center of attention? Even a total stranger you passed on the street or stood in line behind at the grocery store or sat next to in a movie theater. Even fictional characters from books or films. Write down what it was about these people that caught your attention and created your reaction.

From that list, you can begin to formulate ideas for how you can make a stronger impression.

Two cautions, though. First: Don't try to *be* someone else. Don't simply take the behavior of someone you admire and try to make it your own. Be your own person and develop means that feel natural to you. For example, if you're shy, don't try to suddenly become extroverted. It won't work. Find something you can do that works *with* your shyness, such as including a pertinent cartoon in your written correspondence to people. Devise a way to do something extra without trying to tell a joke or drawing attention to yourself, if that makes you uncomfortable.

Second, be sensitive to the line between good taste and bad, between an appreciated gesture and a burdensome exchange. Recognize that the people you are approaching are busy and have many demands on their lives. Be respectful of their time and sensitive to their taste. The man I mentioned above who had a new joke every time I talked to him never told one that was off-color or could be considered racist or sexist. He told them quickly, we shared a laugh, and then we moved right on into the business of our call.

I tell the people who work with me, my sons and daughter, my acquaintances and friends: Don't please people. Provoke them. There is nothing wrong with being provocative.

Remember the scene in *For Whom the Bell Tolls*, with Gary Cooper and Ingrid Bergman, in which the actor Akim Tamiroff says, when taunted by Gary Cooper's character, "I don't provoke, English. I don't provoke. No matter what you say, you can't provoke me." Tamiroff's character hides from the light and cowers from Cooper in order not to provoke attention that might ultimately be harmful. I think the message of that scene is wrong for your purposes. Provoke and provoke again. You are not playing a role in a movie, you *want* to be heard, you *want* to be known, you *want* to be in the light, and you *want* the attention that may ultimately be helpful.

Don't hang back in order to be safe. Don't try to blend in with the decor around you, don't be one more pleasing element in a comfortable background of pleasing elements. Stand out. Be provocative. Make them take notice of you. Create a reaction to get what you want. After all, getting what you want is what living rich is all about.

Fear Only Fear Itself

"The only thing we have to fear is fear itself." Franklin Delano Roosevelt's famous dictum, uttered during the depths of our nation's worst depression, inspired millions of Americans to muster up faith in the country's future. But Roosevelt was not the first, nor the last, nor the most eloquent, to speak on the subject of fear and its effect on our lives. Consider these:

"The thing I fear most is fear." Michel de Montaigne, 1580.

"Nothing is terrible except fear itself." Francis Bacon, 1623.

"The only thing I am afraid of is fear." The Duke of Wellington, 1831.

"Nothing is so much to be feared as fear." Henry Thoreau, 1841.

The consensus is an impressive one, great minds and accomplished personages all in agreement that fear is more detrimental than the object feared. Expounding on the theme to examine the effects of fear, and the way it can negatively affect our pursuit of our dreams, many philosophers and prominent people have further commented as follows:

"Too many people are thinking of security, instead of opportunity. They seem more afraid of life than death." James F. Byrnes.

"There is no security on this earth, there is only opportunity." General Douglas MacArthur.

"Our doubts are traitors, and make us lose the good we oft might win by fearing to attempt." William Shakespeare.

"Fear not that thy life shall come to an end, but rather fear that it shall never have a beginning." Cardinal John Henry Newman.

"Success is a journey, not a destination (see Appendix 5). Happiness is to be found along the way, not at the end of the road, for then the journey is over and it is too late. This day, this hour, this minute is *the* day, *the* hour, *the* minute for each of us to sense the fact that life is good with all of its trials and troubles and perhaps more interesting because of them." Robert R. Updegraff.

"One man with courage makes a majority." Andrew Jackson.

"Is it not strange that we fear most that which never happens? That we destroy our initiative by the fear of defeat when, in reality, defeat is a most useful experience and should be accepted as such." Napoleon Hill.*

Today the simple strength of the message, "There is nothing to fear but fear itself," has new applications in all aspects of life, encouraging people to valiantly face the daily hardships and struggles that assail us all.

*Law of Success—Success Unlimited—Chicago, IL. 1969.

To be without fear would be abnormal; how you handle that fear and adversity is the important issue. Problems and anxieties are everyday occurrences. One person meets these, another person is defeated by them. The difference is attitude. Fear always exists, the question is, will it become your master or will you master your fear? Fear can be crippling, debilitating, paralyzing. Or it can be a source of great focus and inspiration.

We face fear all the time in our lives. Not the huge life-and-death fears of men going into battle and women watching them go. But the everyday fears. Fear of failure, fear of success. Fear of humiliation, fear of rejection. Fear of losing our jobs or of being the victim of a crime or of having an accident. We fear for our children's well-being and we fear the unknown, fear change.

But in almost all instances, the thing we fear is not anywhere near as terrible as the fear itself.

I have found that the amount of fear I have about something is often directly related to how badly I want whatever it is I am afraid of. I believe this is universal. The more you like and are attracted to some person, the more afraid you will probably be to approach him or her. The more you are afraid that you'll be ineffective in making something happen, the more you really want it to occur. The tragedy is that all too often, because our fear increases with our desires, we do not pursue the things that we want most.

The difference between success and failure is the courage of the successful man to act. For remember, a person who tries to do something and fails is better off than the person who tries nothing and succeeds. A person must have the courage to risk making a mistake. Eventually his mistakes will make that person better. You don't want to come to the end of your life regretting the risks you did not take.

Edison failed six thousand times in his attempt to develop the lightbulb. When asked about what he had ultimately accomplished, he simply stated, "I know six thousand ways that you can not develop the lightbulb." He continued until he did see the light. Mistakes can be a great teacher. The single most important factor leading to the end result is your attitude. You can affect your life by changing your attitude. Successful men expect more good out of life than bad. Be positive in your approach. Eliminate the negative. Think big. Don't underestimate. Don't be afraid. Obviously, if you set no goal, if you do not believe you can do something, you can't possibly do it. If you think you can do it, you will do it. Remember, what you can conceive, you can achieve. But if you minimize your own potential out of fear, your potential will be minimal. Only you can determine where you will be in this life, but oddly enough, through the miracle of your own convictions and attitude, you have the ability to be whatever you desire to be.

George Burns said the secret to his good and long life was attitude. His attitude could control any good or bad situation.

Fear gives us the illusion of control. It makes us think that we can avoid the pitfalls and circumstances that will make us feel bad. But this thinking is both erroneous and circular.

To begin with, we can't control the universe. No matter how vigilant our fear makes us think we are being, life will blindside us. As we discussed in an earlier chapter, stuff happens. And in my experience, it is the people who are listening most closely to their fears, the ones who think they are prepared for every exigency, who are most devastated when the reality inevitably hits. They bank so hard on being in control that they are completely unprepared when they inevitably realize that life is beyond their command.

Furthermore, by trying to avoid things we are afraid of, what we really do is avoid things we want in order to not risk losing them. If you think about it, you'll realize that this doesn't make any sense. To avoid losing something of value, we don't risk getting it, so we have "lost" it anyway. We deny ourselves the thing we want so that we won't have to worry that it will be taken away. It's a matter of no guts, no glory or, as *Forbes* magazine always says, "No guts, no story."

Look at it this way: Jim would like to date a movie star. But he is afraid that if he asks her out she will reject him. To avoid this rejection, he doesn't ask her out. Therefore, he doesn't date her. He denies himself his goal to avoid her denying it to him. And the saddest part is that, because so many men may think this way, the beautiful movie star may only rarely be asked out, and may just be waiting for someone real to come along.

This is what fear does to our lives. It is one of the biggest obstacles to living rich.

Often we mistake our fear for a more reasoned decision. An investment opportunity comes along. It's exciting, with great potential rewards, but risky. In evaluating the investment, we may unknowingly determine it to be unsound not because the prospectus doesn't check out, but because we are afraid of the risk. There is nothing wrong with caution (see Appendix 4), but it is good to know the real reasons we make the choices we make. That way, if we are making them out of fear, we can reassess them on a more substantial basis. If indeed it turns out that we have nothing to fear but fear itself, we may be missing out on a wealth of wonderful, life-enriching opportunities.

No one is free of fear. It assaults us all. But there are techniques that allow some people to overcome their fears, to use the fear to actually help further their goals. Fear produces adrenaline, and adrenaline is stimulation that you can turn to creativity and problem-solving. You can use it to your advantage if you aren't afraid of being afraid. Fear is good. Barbra Streisand and many other major performers admit to having butterflies in their stomachs before going onstage. Once again, the fact that their adrenaline is pumping helps give them the energy and drive to produce a better or even superior performance.

One of the editors I have worked with on various projects told me that she tends to be very shy and easily intimidated in new situations and for many years had allowed her fear to keep her from going places and doing things she very much wanted to do. Finally she realized that she was letting her fright run her life. Determined to overcome the obstacle of her fear, she adopted it as a battle cry, a rallying call to her will. When she approached a new situation and felt the old fear creeping up, instead of giving in to it or backing down, she conjured an up an image of herself mounted on horseback, leading a cavalry charge, carrying the battalion flag into battle. And as she spurred her horse forward she sat up straight in the saddle and yelled, *"Scared!"* as her signal to charge forth into the fray. She knew that she was scared, accepted the fact, but accorded it no more importance than she might give to any other curious but nonlethal observation. Soon she was going out more and more often, until eventually she realized she'd gotten so strong she didn't need the battle cry anymore.

I have a similar technique that I employ when fear threatens to overwhelm me. I do a countdown in my head of the most dire possible outcomes of my activity, the worst things that could happen as a result. If the progression doesn't end with some irrevocable tragedy, I know my fear is disproportionate. For example, let's say you are afraid of public speaking and have been asked to address a professional association. What's the worst thing that could happen? You could botch the speech. What's the worst that could happen if you did? Some people might laugh or think less of you. Most won't, most will be understanding and sympathetic and encouraging—in my experience, people really are mostly good. But some could laugh. So you have gotten information about the people in your association, you know who is cruel and thoughtless and who is kind and generous. These are good things to know. Maybe the ones who ridicule you will not want to do business with you in the future. So what—you don't really need them, do you? You won't lose your job over it, you won't be out on the streets, no one will die. Bottom line, nothing all that terrible is going to happen and some good things very likely might. So what is there, really, to be afraid of except the fear itself? Fear must always be put into perspective. Everything exists in relation to everything else and perspective can bring back reality.

A young student away at school flunked two of her classes and feared her parents' wrath. Out of her fear, she wrote them the following note:

Dear Mom and Dad,

My skull fracture is slowly healing, as is the concussion that came with the fracture when I jumped out of the window when my room caught fire. I was in the hospital for three weeks, which is why you haven't heard from me, but I am feeling much better now except for the migraine headaches I suffer. But I only get those two or three times a day anymore, so things are much improved.

I always thought John and I got a little too high

from the pot we were smoking; I guess I was right because that's how the room caught fire, making us have to jump out of the window. And I would have written sooner except that this broken arm makes it difficult, none of which really matters, since I'm planning to quit school anyway.

Stu, my friend from India, decided to take care of me during my convalescence. He and I are now madly in love and are planning to get married. The wedding will almost certainly take place before my pregnancy begins to show. He has been offered a good job in Alaska, where there is a particularly active branch of Alcoholics Anonymous, which should help him resolve his drinking problem. We are simply waiting for the infection he had and then gave to me to clear up; the doctors feel fairly certain that this new drug we're trying will do the trick. As soon as that happens, we will be leaving. However, we might be delayed since he has to make sure his wife doesn't create too many problems for us.

I will keep you posted.

Love,

Me

P.S. None of the above is really true. However, I did receive a D in English and an F in Geometry and I thought it was best to put these grades into proper perspective for you.

The student turned her fear to her advantage and used it to create an approach that was a problem-solver instead of problem-maker. By bringing everything into perspective for herself she was able to voice that perspective to her parents and turn her fear into an ally.

Fear feeds upon itself. By causing the result you are afraid you will get, the fear nourishes itself and reinforces its dire message. But your dreams needn't be food for the active growth of your fears. You can feed upon the fear instead of letting it feed upon you.

One of the truly tragic outcomes of a fearfully lived life is regret. Regret for missed opportunities, regret for unfulfilled dreams, regret for unused potential.

I knew a man who went on a vacation and had an opportunity to go scuba diving among the exquisite coral reefs around Mexico's Cozumel island. Frightened to don the mask and breathing apparatus, the man passed on the chance. But it bothered him for a long, long time. The vision of the colorful fish and delicate corals and the exclamations of the other members of his group who had gone down with the dive master stayed with him and ate at him.

"It's driving me crazy, Barry," he told me. "I saw those other people go down and come back up safely and so happily excited. Worse, I really wanted to do it. That's what gets me. I had the chance and I really wanted to take it and I let myself be frightened and intimidated into missing it."

Eventually, the only thing that would appease his regret was to go back on another vacation and join the group for the diving experience.

He was still exclaiming about it when he returned and we next spoke. "It was amazing, Barry! So quiet and beautiful. To be a part of this whole other world filled with all these wonders, it was incredible!"

"And weren't you afraid?" I asked.

"I was, some, at first. But you know what? I found I was much more frightened of living with that regret than I was of taking the risk. I'll never forget how it stayed with me, made me think less of myself. I kept seeing the march of days in my life and imagining how it would feel to get to the end of them and have regrets about things I could have done differently. It was an awful feeling. I don't ever want to feel like that again."

The next I heard, the man was taking scuba lessons and was going to get certified.

A few years later, the same man was touring Egypt. When he came back, he told me that he'd almost passed on a chance to go into one of the great pyramids until he remembered his previous experience with missed opportunities.

"I was standing in line waiting my turn to go into the pyramid," he said, "and, as I got closer, I got more and more apprehensive.

"You enter through this small, narrow, dark tunnel that plunges almost straight down into the ground under unimaginable tons of solid rock. You can't even stand up straight, you have to crouch all the way down, and there are so many people going in and out that you're virtually trapped in place. It was quite daunting.

"I was going to get out of line and pass on the whole thing when I suddenly remembered what it felt like when I got back from Cozumel that first time. It occurred to me that when I came to regret missing this opportunity I'd have to travel all the way back to Egypt to make it up! That was enough to get me to go," he laughed.

"Frankly," he concluded, "there wasn't much to see in there and I wouldn't have missed much if I hadn't gone, but what I gained by overcoming the fear and making a determined grab for the opportunity is immeasurable."

I've thought about that story a lot. Thought about the terrible possibility of reaching the end of one's life and looking back with regret on the chances not taken. It *is* an awful prospect, far more frightening than trying and failing. I have made a mental note to remember, when I'm afraid of trying something, how much more severe the idea of dying with regrets is. This technique has helped me undertake some of the most fun and exhilarating—and profitable—experiences of my life.

"The only thing in this life that I regret are the risks I did not take." I think of this when I have decisions to make, to remind myself not to make a choice out of fear that might prevent me from pursuing something I really want. It reinforces my perspective.

Some fear is healthy. Had the man speaking above not been dealing with a reputable diving company that employed numerous safeguards in taking novices under the water, his fear might have saved his life. There are real dangers out there and it's good to be alert to them.

But most of the time the things we fear on a day-to-day basis are not matters of life and death. Their most dire possible outcome is embarrassment or failure. Or further fear. Listening to those fears and allowing them to stop us from experiencing life fully impoverishes us to the same degree that overcoming them enriches us.

Think about the things you are afraid of and how that fear affects your decisions and lifestyle. Make a list of the fears and their effects. Then make a list of things you would like to do if only you weren't afraid. Write down how you would be different if you weren't afraid, how you appear to yourself when you imagine yourself engaging in those activities without the fear. Using your imagination, draw a picture of your fear and put it inside a circle with a line through it. Keep that picture posted somewhere you would usually be when the fear crops up: in your car, in your briefcase, on your desk, on your refrigerator. Resolve to undertake one thing you have been afraid to do, whether it's a recreational activity, a professional pursuit, or an emotionally healing process such as attempting a reconciliation with someone from whom you are estranged. Feed on your fear, make it work *for* you in leading you to the things that are most important and most rewarding. There is no feeling quite as powerful as doing something despite being afraid of it, or *because* you are afraid of it, and triumphing.

Then watch and rejoice as, freed from the controlling influence of your fears, your life opens to a wealth of new possibilities.

13

Focus on the Long View for the Shortest Path

Y ou are going to be dead much longer than you'll be alive. Waste not one moment, for it can never be regained. Leave no word unsaid. Live, enjoy, live rich.

When selling insurance, it is difficult not to become philosophical about life . . . and death. I see the suddenness with which illness and death can strike, I know firsthand from hundreds of personal experiences with my clients how devastating the losses can be. How unfinished lives can be. I have seen the tragedy of wasted lives over and over again, heard far too many stories of deathbed regrets. It never fails to hurt and sadden me.

I've learned from these experiences to savor life. To regard every moment of it as precious, wonderful, and useful. I hear great wisdom in all the contemporary slogans that exhort us to "stop and smell the roses," "live each day as if it were your last," "live in and for the moment," "take life one day at a time."

One of my clients was speaking to me after having suffered a near-death experience. He told me of a transformation in his attitude that had occurred as a result of this, a transformation that is said to be common among people who come close to death.

"I feel so grateful to be alive," he said. "Not in the sense of being thankful that I didn't die, but in a far more important way." He struggled to put into words feelings that were obviously very new and very deep. "Life has become such a treasure, Barry. Everything about it is so good. As if my senses were newly vital and my attention newly focused upon them. Everything—*everything*—brings me such joy."

I think it's sad that he had to go through such a painful and frightening process to reach this happy conclusion. Sadder still, I'm afraid that none of us who hasn't gone through the same process can really appreciate the depth of what he was feeling. It is too easy to take life for granted until we come face to face with losing it.

So I try to remember these lessons throughout my days. If you come to my office and are meeting with me at a time when one of my grandchildren stops in, you can expect our meeting to be briefly interrupted while I attend to the important business of loving that child. If my wife calls from our museum, I will always take the call. I have identified my priorities, the things that make everything else worthwhile. What would success be without my wife and family to share it with? What is wealth without the joy of using it to see and do things and enjoy my children and grandchildren?

Those are the moments that make my life rich.

With that said, I'm going to change tracks completely to

talk about the need for long-range planning, ambition, and a long view.

It may seem contradictory for me to exhort the wonders of life's individual moments and then tell you that you need to look and plan far ahead, but to me these two concepts are not mutually exclusive but mutually beneficial. One does not negate the other, they work in tandem.

Perhaps I can explain it this way. I would love my grand-children no matter what our personal circumstances, and I believe they would love me regardless of the material benefits I could lavish upon them. In love there is a great and simple joy. But I like being able to treat them well. I like knowing that my life's work means they will have advantages and opportunities they might not otherwise have enjoyed. It helps give my life purpose and a sense of meaning. And I don't think I'm unusual in this. To leave life better for the generations of families that come after us is, I believe, a pretty common goal.

To get to the point where I could fulfill all the aspects of my dreams for my grandchildren and myself, I had to look beyond the moment, or the day, or the week, month, or year. I had to think in broad, sweeping terms, to have a vision that has spanned virtually my whole adult life. Ambition, determination, dreaming—they are all future-based. They all aim ahead and hope and plan for something more or dif-ferent.

It's like the outline for this book that my cowriter pre-pared for us to work from. I gave her the concepts I wanted to espouse, my ideas, my thoughts, and my overviews. She delineated the chapters, determined their order, and broke down what each one would accomplish and how it would contribute to the whole. That would be the long-range plan. Then, on what would be a day-to-day basis, we filled in the words, told the stories, gave flesh to the skeleton. While we never lost sight of the desired end, never quit working toward the final product, along the way there were memories shared and turns of phrase appreciated and pleasure in the process. I rewrote it two times and she re-edited it three.

I still believe life is a destination, but I don't think that has to preclude you from enjoying the journey as you go.

Too many people see only the next chore ahead of them, plan only the day they have awakened into. In my experience, these people get nowhere except to the next day. I don't believe it is possible to live richly without having a goal, a purpose that enlivens you.

I spoke earlier about Dan Jansen and his long-awaited Olympic triumph. Think about the special joy of potential fulfilled and abilities realized and ambitions achieved that his story represents. He trained on a daily basis for years and years to achieve the one moment that would shine in his life above all else.

Do you have a personal goal? And has it become an obsession? If so, you know how working toward it can enliven you. If not, you should try to find such a goal. It need not be anything grandiose or publicly noteworthy. The specifics are unimportant. It is having the goal that matters.

My wife Carole and I started to seriously collect miniatures four years ago. As do all dedicated collectors, we became addicted and obsessed. But this obsession brought a new dimension to our lives. New goals and purposes, and certainly a new exquisiteness to living rich. This was the youth we had missed, dolls and doll houses, trains, planes, and cars. Fancy furnishings and whimsical settings. Imagination free to create whatever it conceived.

Now I visit my wife's museum every weekend simply to "play with all my toys." I am completely fulfilled, my wife has allowed me to live vicariously through sharing her obsession and her incredible ability to bring it to its total fruition. What joy this is! What a mass of riches to be shared with all who come to enjoy our collection. It was once said that "he who dies with the most toys, wins." I am not concerned with dying with the most toys. I am too busy enjoying my life; for remember it is never too late to have a happy childhood.

Another woman I know was also yearning for things she missed in her youth. She'd wanted to be popular and active and to have a wide circle of friends, but for various reasons these things had always eluded her. Now in her mid-sixties, her children safe and grown, her time more available, she is finally satisfying those old desires. She tells me she is happier then she's ever been. Her dream was not an earthshaking one, not momentous to anyone but her. But nonetheless it has great power.

Make a list of the things you would like from your life. Be specific. "I want to have children," "I want to sail the world for a year," "I want to be famous," "I want to be rich," "I want to be elected to office," "I want to be a collector."

Now make a second list of steps that would lead to the accomplishment of that goal, the necessary process entailed in realizing the dream. Then make a third list of things you are or could be doing to reach your goal. You are now ready to begin the first day of the rest of your life.

What these lists should come to reveal is an ever-longer focus of purpose. You start with the day-to-day things that will bring you in incremental steps to the ultimate fulfillment of your goal. Along the way, you enjoy the pleasure and pride of accomplishing each step. Your life is full with the ebullience of knowing you are creating movement toward something you greatly desire.

This is what makes life rich and worth living.

Practice taking the long view. Get up in the morning, review what your day holds in store, and identify those steps that are helping you achieve your greater goal. If there aren't any, find a way to incorporate them. Days go by quickly and life doesn't wait for us to make time. Also, look for those things that may be working against you. Are you in a job that offers no chance of supporting your ultimate purpose? If so, *now* is the best time to start looking for the way out and into something better. Just bringing home a paycheck may support your lifestyle today, but it won't necessarily help you get anywhere you really want to be.

Are there classes you could be taking, seminars you could be attending, contacts you could be making? Have you been putting off writing the proposal or making the call that is the next step on your list? Think about what you are waiting for. Chances are it will never happen unless you *make* it happen. When you make major decisions in your life (see Appendix 4), think about how they will affect your process.

Rhonda Morstein, cowriter of this book and contributing editor of three of my previous books, told me of her personal experience with allowing herself to be deflected from her desired path.

"I always wanted to be a writer. I went to college, got a degree in creative writing with the desire to someday be a published author.

"But I was afraid to pursue the dream. How would I live until my writing began to bring me income? I was unwilling to take the risk and devote the energy. So I got a job as a copywriter at an advertising agency, and I did well at it. I didn't make much money, but it was enough to get by and I had time to write in the evenings, so I was happy.

"Before too long the boss offered me a promotion to project director. It meant a considerable raise and I thought that was what I was supposed to want, so I took it. But I had to *earn* that additional money, and doing so kept me working longer hours, sometimes taking work home. The responsibility weighed more heavily upon me, and what off time I did have felt less free.

"Over the next fourteen years this pattern continued. I worked my way up and up within the advertising industry, earning more and more money, bringing home more and more awards. Every time a promotion or advancement was offered to me, I took it thinking I would be foolish to turn down such good fortune.

"But now I was working sixty-five to seventy hours a week. I was contributing some of my evenings to a professional association to make new contacts, and I was spending at least one weekend day touring clients' projects. The added income had gone to buy a more expensive car and a condominium that demanded more upkeep, which cost more money.

"I never wrote anymore. I was an executive. We had staff to do the copywriting and I had neither the time nor the strength to write at home. I had lost sight of my dream.

"Only luck brought Barry and me together to work on his first book. And I almost blew that. I was so busy with other things that I missed our first deadline, and Barry told me that if I wasn't dedicated to the project he would have to give it to someone else. Suddenly I felt a sense of panic and I *knew* how very intensely I was devoted to writing. Even though it wasn't my project, it wouldn't put my name on an index card in the Library of Congress, it was closer than anything I had let myself do in years and years.

"I convinced Barry to give me a second chance. *Live Rich* is our fourth project together. I've completed a novel, as yet unpublished, but, oh, what a joyous sense of accomplishment! And I am almost through with another personal project. I live much more frugally and simply, but I am happier than I ever was making the big dollars and winning the awards and moving up the rungs of the corporate ladder, because I am working toward *my* goals for *my* benefit. I feel that each day of my life moves me toward the place I had always wanted to be. I'm looking ahead now, seeing a future filled with possibility instead of only seeing as far ahead as the next meeting or ad deadline. And what I see thrills me."

If you look down the line of your current path, where does it lead you? Will you be happy at that destination? More important, if tragedy struck and you found out you had only a month to live, would you be happy with where you have been? It is one thing to regret being cheated out of the time or opportunity to see your goal come to fruition. It is another thing entirely to realize that you cheated yourself by not doing everything you could to get there while you had the chance. This, I think, is the near-death lesson, the blend of living for today and realizing that today leads to tomorrow.

It is easy to get lost in the wilderness of daily demands. That's why it is so important to start at the end, to define your destination and then plot backward the path you need to take to get there. In this way, each day of your life is imbued with meaning. Use a long lens, and take a lot of snapshots along the way, and your focus will be definitive. Focus on the long view and you will find it to be the shortest path to your destination.

Remember, focus and concentration are mandatory to achievement. To live rich and enjoy life requires such a silent, subtle concentration and focus.

A tree stands for hundreds of years and produces no smoke, but hold a magnifying glass between the sun and its bark and it will begin smoking in seconds. Only such focus can ignite the potential in each and every one of your dreams.

Invest in Success

"Put your money where your mouth is!" As kids we delighted in urging a braggart to back up his claim. "Put up or shut up," we'd tease.

It was an effective technique. You could immediately tell when someone was telling the truth, or believed he was. He wouldn't hesitate to meet any stake.

I learned a lot from those boyhood interactions. Nowadays I can still judge someone who is certain of his position by his willingness to "put up or shut up."

Media people call me all the time, as do specialty advertising firms, wanting me to use their venue for my promotions. They tell me how certain they are that I will get great results and often even quote figures for an anticipated percentage of return. I always ask them the same thing: "Will you give me back my money if I don't get the results you promise?" After all, if they're really so positive, my request shouldn't present much of a gamble. But they almost never accept my challenge. And that tells me that they're not as sure as they'd like to be. They are willing to risk my money but they're not willing to risk their own. Needless to say, I rarely do business under those circumstances.

I apply the same lesson in reverse to my own business practices. If I'm going to make a claim, I back it up with a tangible offering of proof. In my industry, the law prohibits guarantees about the cost of products or their eventual returns because these things are controlled by the insurance companies and determined by changes in mortality and interest rates. But I do, for example, offer to review any prospect's needs and provide a free proposal, because I am pretty certain that I will be able to show them how to maximize their insurance expenditures so efficiently that they will be inclined to do business with me. If I can't save them any money or optimize their coverage and assets, there is no charge for my services in making that determination.

I put my money where my mouth is and make an investment in my time and energy. Only through this investment can I realize any success.

People respond to this degree of certainty, just as I would be inclined to try a new medium if the rep would guarantee me the results he so blithely predicts. I get so many requests for proposals that it takes a whole staff to process them. And from this volume of new business prospects, I have built one of the country's most successful insurance operations and my own fortune.

Investing in your success is a critical aspect of attaining your dreams. The fact is, if you're not willing to invest in yourself, why should someone else be? The investment need not be financial. It could come in the form of time or energy or material goods, but if you won't be the first to back up your plan, proposal, or project with an investment of some kind, how could you expect someone else to? I put my money where my mouth is. I have a very substantial amount of life insurance; more than most of my clients. I commit to every one of my clients that I will do no less for him or her than I have done for my own family. I demonstrate my belief by living it every day.

When I wrote my second book, *Save a Fortune on Your Estate Taxes*, I found getting someone to publish it was very difficult. I'm sure most authors have had this problem. Limited in the number of books they can publish a year, limited in the amount of money they will spend to promote those books, the publishing industry can appear shortsighted and impossible to break into. But I was pretty certain that there was a market for my book. After all, almost everyone buys insurance at some point in his life, and very few people really understand the product they are buying. So I published the book myself. It cost me a significant amount of money to do so, and given the publishing world's rejections, it represented a risk. But I believed in the book, believed in myself, and was willing to demonstrate that belief in the only tangible manner available to me.

Save a Fortune on Your Estate Taxes went on to become one of the all-time best-selling books on the subject. Several years later, in fact, Business Irwin One, a division of the Times Mirror Company, approached me to do an updated paperback version, which I did.

Nor did I stop with the initial investment of publishing my own books. When my third book, *Die Rich and Tax Free*, was published and distributed to bookstores, I found that it wasn't being promoted or displayed in an efficient manner. So I undertook to promote it myself. I ran ads at my own expense, mentioned and sold it at all my seminars, included it in promotional materials for other products. The direct sales of the book, for which I make over two times the return I do on bookstore sales, approaches three times greater volume. I had to invest in the advertising expenses, fulfillment personnel, the packaging and mailing materials, but it was well worth it. Because I was willing to take the risk and invest in the success of the project, I was able to make it a success. Whereas the bookstores, who made no major investments, reaped much less reward. Of course, they make up for it with the volume of books they handle.

Investment almost always equals risk. And risk is troublesome, even dangerous. We all feel that way; no one is immune. No matter how equipped we are to absorb a loss, there is some part of ourselves tied up in not losing.

But just as investment almost always equals risk, risk can very often be the sole means to reward.

Bob, whom I keep returning to as an example because of the simple, heartfelt joy his story provokes in me, invested his time and creative energies and imagination and *heart* in his pursuit of Marsha. He had to risk rejection and embarrassment to do so. But the reward of her hand in marriage was well worth it.

George Foreman invested his time and his body and his spirit in pursuing that heavyweight championship. He risked public failure and the crushing of his dreams. But the reward was a moment in time, a triumph of will, that he will never forget.

Daniel Day-Lewis invested his energy and his determination to master the role of Christy Brown. He risked his health and his pride of accomplishment. As a reward, he earned an Oscar.

All achievement requires an investment. You must be willing to put up.

Someone will not descend into your life, determine your dreams to be worthy, and take it upon himself to make them happen. Life is not a fairy tale. If you wait for someone else to discover you, you will most likely die unknown.

Most people think of investing in themselves in financial terms. And certainly, those terms apply. Being willing to risk your own money to further an idea—to produce an invention, start a business, manufacture a product—will probably be critical to making that idea or product or business a success. Even if you can get a loan, it will be a loan *against* something, some piece of collateral that you must be willing to risk.

But money, in my opinion, is the least difficult thing to invest. You may think that because I am wealthy it is easy for me to contemplate risking money. But one doesn't arrive at my financial status without valuing a dollar and knowing its worth. Still, I know that the means for making money exist all around me. It is, after all, just another commodity. The really difficult things for most people to invest are the far more precious commodities of time, energy, and one's belief in oneself.

Back on the playground, if the braggart who was challenged to "put your money where your mouth is" was too afraid to take the bet, the repercussions were brutal. He was jeered and derided. For days, he was the butt of jokes and taunts, and some piece of the stigma was carried with him for a long time.

It is no less brutal a risk to put yourself forward as an adult. It still takes a lot of courage to trot your wares into the marketplace and put them up for sale. You have to do so with the full belief that they are of value and you have to do so knowing that the shoppers in the market might well laugh at what you offer.

But when the braggart *would* take the bet, a hush would fall. As his dirty hand would reach defiantly forward to proffer the shiny dime or quarter he was willing to stake, the other kids were impressed. That he would invest not so much his money in the bet but his credibility, his standing in the hierarchy, his stature, elevated the boy and validated his claim simply by virtue of his willingness to back it up.

We have not progressed very much from the schoolyard children we once were. The clothes are different, the stakes different, the investment vehicle is different, but we still put our credibility, our stature, and our position on the line each time we step out and make a claim about ourselves, each time we assert ourselves, or our wares, to be deserving.

And it is still this risk that offers the greatest hope for reward. The bankers you approach for a loan, the client to whom you make the proposal, the love interest you pursue, is also still the young schoolyard child who will be hushed and impressed when you thrust out your hand and reveal the shiny dime or quarter clutched in your palm.

It is often said that all anyone ever has is fifteen minutes of glory in a lifetime—his or her fifteen minutes in the sun—Andy Warhol's infamous "fifteen minutes of fame." Using the techniques I have espoused in *Live Rich*, I believe you will be able to secure a much longer time. You can create and sustain for yourself a foundation that will be more than large enough to support a whole lifetime of living rich.

Success Is Learned, Not Taught

J ust as it is unlikely that anyone is going to magically appear and take it upon himself to promote your dreams and make them come true for you, it is just as unlikely that someone is going to make it his business to teach you all you need to know about your chosen path.

Some people assert that I may have taught many in my industry everything they know. But I have not taught them everything *I* know. No one does; you have to learn for yourself.

A friend with whom I was discussing this chapter told me a story that I think perfectly illustrates this point.

"When I was about ten years old," he said, "my father gave me the chore of painting the bare walls of our basement. He handed me a big paintbrush, the kind the professional painters used, and a couple of gallons of white paint, and told me to get to work.

"I liked it in the basement. It was cool and dim and mechanical things made noises and there were smells and shapes that I could imagine were all sorts of things. And the painting was fun. I lavished paint on the wall, imagined I was some great artist producing a valuable and much-acclaimed new work. I painted in broad, slashing strokes; pirate sword-fight strokes, lion-tamer strokes.

"But when I was done and the paint had dried the wall looked terrible! My sweeping, daring brush strokes had left it looking like a patchwork quilt. And my father was not happy.

"He told me to do it over and 'this time, do it right!'

" 'But I didn't know,' I protested. 'You didn't tell me there was a right way or a wrong one.'

" 'You didn't ask me,' was my father's simple, inarguable answer, spoken gently but carrying a strong message. 'You didn't ask me, and you didn't find out for yourself. It was your job to do, not mine.'

"Still he didn't tell me what I'd done wrong. I had to figure it out for myself. But I didn't want to risk having to paint a *third* coat, so I walked down to the hardware store and asked the owner. He showed me the proper way to hold the brush and to apply the paint in even, vertical strokes.

"I listened, watched, and learned. And the second time painting that basement was the last time.

"The lesson stuck with me, too. I never again relied on someone else to tell me what or how to do something. I realized that I had to learn for myself what I needed to know."

In any endeavor you undertake, you will encounter things you do not know. Everyone has to start somewhere. And though guidance will often be available, there are some things no one can teach you. Things you will simply have to learn for yourself. Asking questions is fine, but often you don't even know that you should be questioning something. It never occurred to my friend to ask his father *how* to paint the basement walls; he had no idea there was any technique involved. But he learned, as have I, that the first thing to do in approaching any new situation is to avoid making assumptions and to question everything.

In school I was taught a lot of things. But I find the only stuff I remember is the stuff I *learned*. I could memorize lessons, repeat back to the teacher the things he or she wanted to hear. But it was only when I dug into something, when I explored it, investigated it, followed the track of it, that I made it my own.

And it was the lessons I made my own that enriched my purpose. To this day, the same holds true. What I am taught, I take somewhat for granted. What I *learn*, I hold dear.

I do not hesitate to guess that you are the same way. Most everybody I have met and talked with is. Being taught is a very passive exercise, it's not particularly engaging or compelling. But learning is an active process that enlivens and invigorates us.

Don't hesitate to pursue learning. Don't assume you know it all. More important, don't assume the other person knows it all. Employ a scientific process of trial and error to learn for yourself what works and what doesn't.

Rhonda tells of the first time she was hired in her advertising copywriter capacity to write a television commercial script.

"We'd done the print advertising for this client's product for many years very successfully. We'd developed a whole campaign for him. Then cable television came along and made broadcast a financially viable addition for his marketing plan, so we decided to translate the print campaign into a commercial.

"I'd never written a script for television. But I didn't want to tell the client that because I feared he'd pull the job, and I was confident of my concept for the commercial.

"What I didn't do, however, was stop to consider that the format of writing scripts was entirely different from that for writing print copy. And the client didn't know either; it was his first foray into broadcast and he was relying on me.

"When we handed the document to the producer who would be making the spot for us, he looked puzzled. 'Haven't you ever done this before?' he asked me. I stammered some excuse. The client was furious. I'd made him look foolish, as if he were too simple to realize his agency didn't know what it was doing. I was humiliated and very nearly lost the account simply because I hadn't thought to question my assumptions.

"There are books out there that show you in detail how to format manuscripts for all different kinds of media. All I had to do was think beyond my assumptions. Question. And learn."

Of course, Rhonda could have asked someone to teach her how to format her script, but there is a danger in that. Namely, how do you know that the person you're consulting really knows? Often it's a risk too big to take.

When I had just started out in the insurance industry, I was preparing some paperwork for submission to a potential insurer on behalf of a client to whom I had never had to submit before. It was a complex form having to do with a complicated estate plan, and I was unsure how best to proceed. So I asked one of the other agents who worked in the same office, and he walked me through the process. I followed his lead, completed the forms, and sent them to the insurer for a quote. A few days later I got a call from a representative of the insurer. The paperwork was all wrong and would need to be redone. It wasn't the end of the world, although it did delay my ability to respond in a timely fashion to my client's request.

I should have called the insurer immediately when I realized I didn't understand the form. I should have had the insurer explain to me exactly what was wanted. I didn't even bother to ask my coworker if he'd ever had to fill out this particular form before. (When I went back to him and showed him his errors, he admitted to me that he'd never dealt with that request before and had just been doing his best. He'd been afraid, he admitted, to reveal that he didn't know what to do.) I just assumed that since he'd been there longer than I had, he knew better.

After the insurer walked me through the process, I *never* forgot!

What are the ten most important things you don't know about *your* business or project and have been too frightened, reluctant, or lazy to find out? Make a list and then write down where you could go to find the answers. Remember, sometimes the best answer lies in trial and error as opposed to reading or asking some third party.

Of course, these examples make the process seem easy. You're undertaking a task, you research for yourself the best way to proceed, and then you employ what you learned. Simple.

But life is rarely simple. And the majority of the time, the things you need to learn will not be cut-and-dried formulas. What you usually need to learn is individual and personal; the best way for you to proceed is not necessarily the same as the best way for someone else. In which case, the only means to learning is trial and error.

I could tape-record one of my seminars and have the dialogue transcribed and give the script to one of my sons to memorize. They are both in the business with me, both extremely knowledgeable and capable. Yet even so, even using my exact words and my exact pacing and my exact intonation, they would not get the same results as I do. The lack of their own connection to what they were saying would be noticeable and people would be put off.

However, either of my sons could present the same material I do in his own words and his own manner and might easily surpass my results.

Your individuality is what makes someone favor you over everyone else. It's one of your greatest commodities in the pursuit of your desires. No one can teach you how to best exercise that uniqueness. That's something you must learn for yourself.

In creative writing classes, students are taught how to utilize metaphors, how to structure and balance complex and simple sentences, how to create dialogue. They are advised to "write what they know" and be descriptive. Anyone taking the classes could learn these lessons. Yet few will become great writers. For that to occur, individuality must be expressed. The writer must find his or her unique voice and transcend the lessons to produce something rare and special.

Actors can be taught how to project their voices, how to walk in the manner of a certain character, how to count the beats of a dramatic pause. But they can't be taught how to emote. That special ability comes from within.

The only way to polish your special ability, to perfect the craft of your ambition, is by learning for yourself. No one can teach you how best to be you. You must be willing to risk trial and error, to experiment.

There is no teacher like experience: Success is learned, not taught. Experience equates with learning. No teacher— nothing taught to you—will prove as useful as the learning experiences you embrace. Whatever it is you are setting out to do, keep in mind that each attempt you make is providing you with vital information. Don't get discouraged if your first attempt doesn't net the desired result, or if the third, fifth, or tenth still has not provided complete fulfillment. Each of those attempts reaps something just as valuable: lessons in what does and does not work. From those, you can eliminate that which is not contributing to your success and focus on that which is. You can learn.

I have had as many "failures" as I have had successes in building and developing my business (I use the quotation marks around "failures" because while outsiders may deem the end result of some of my attempts as unsuccessful, I do not see them as such). Some of these were quite costly—on paper. But I've noticed that, without exception, the lessons I learned matched or exceeded in value whatever toll they exacted. By daring to fail, I dared to win. And as time has gone by and the lessons my attempts taught me have been assimilated into my overall comprehension and planning, I win a lot more often than I don't. The same is true within my personal life and family structure.

Only through failure can there be success. We can only learn from our failures. Failures are actually an integral part of success. Michael Jordan must miss the basket 40 percent of the time in order to score 60 percent. Baseball's top hitters strike out a goodly percentage of their at-bats. You could consider that this means they have to fail some percentage of the time in order to succeed the rest of the time. Dan Marino can successfully pass only six out of ten attempts. But each failure brings him closer to the next success and helps guarantee that success. If Michael Jordan or Dan Marino didn't attempt so much, they couldn't succeed so much. If they didn't try, they couldn't win. And if they didn't learn from their mistakes, they would never be superstars.

Success is a state of mind. Only with a proper mind-set can you experience a rich life.

Consider the following poem, entitled *How to Build a Hero**:

> If you think you are beaten, you are.
>
> If you think you dare not, you won't.
>
> If you like to win, but you think you can't, it's almost a cinch you won't.
>
> If you think that you'll lose, you've lost.
>
> For out in this world we find success begins with a person's will.
>
> It's all in the state of mind.
>
> If you think that you're outclassed, you are.
>
> You've got to think high to rise.
>
> You've got to be sure of yourself before you can ever win a prize.
>
> Life's battle doesn't always go to the swifter or faster man, but sooner or later the man who wins is the man who thinks he can.

What you think about will come about; whatever it is you desire, you must see yourself doing it, imagine it as having already happened, write it out, act it out. By believing in what we think about and learning what to do with that belief, we bring about that which we hold most dear. James Arch, a public speaker on motivation, quotes William James on this same topic: "The greatest discovery of my generation is that human beings can alter their lives by altering their minds."

*Source unknown.

Have you ever done something you'd never done before and had it not turn out as you'd hoped or expected? Of course you have—we all have. The vacation that just didn't live up to your plans or the date that didn't work out or the job you thought was perfect but was revealed as a total mismatch. There are, in my experience, only two ways of facing these "failures." You can be defeated and vow never to go on another vacation or another date or risk changing your safe existing job for something better again. Or you can take what happened, learn the lesson it had to teach you, and use it to make your next vacation, date, or job even better. No one can teach you these things, no one can know for you what will work, what won't, or what will satisfy you. You can only *learn* these things, they cannot be taught.

When you know what it is that you want from your life, make it your business to find out exactly how to get it. Don't wait for someone to teach you, don't rely on a mentor or friend or loved one to provide you the answers. Find out whatever it is you need to know. Take each and every assumption you hold about your path and test it, research it, try to disprove it. Pursue the knowledge you will need vigorously and as if your life depended on it, for the *quality* of your life very well may. Learn how to fill out the forms, learn how to paint the wall, learn how to format the document. And learn what it is about yourself that holds you back or gives you an edge. Explore your world, your place in it, and the process by which it can be shaped to fit your desire.

16

Be Born Again

My walk will be different and my name,
nothing is goin' to be the same,
I'm goin' to change my way of living,
if that ain't enough,
then I'll change the way I strut my stuff*.

hese lyrics, from the song "There'll Be Some Changes
Made," fill me with a joyful sort of hope. The voice in
which they are uttered seems to be proud and defiant and
determined. And the words embody my own belief that
change is an exercise of will and that we all have the ability,
at any time, to simply alter those things we are not happy
with if only we will dare to do so.

*Edward B. Marks Music Company—New York, NY. 1921.

Six years ago, my wife Carole decided that she wanted to change her life. Nothing drastic was necessary; she wasn't really unhappy. She simply felt that she needed to make some change that would revitalize her and give her a fresh outlook. So she added an *e* to her name. Carol became Carole and her whole life changed. Whether the change was apparent to her friends or colleagues was unimportant. What mattered was that it changed the way she saw herself from that point on. She was no longer Carol who had gotten into the habit of doing certain things a certain way. Now she was Carole and free to reinvent herself or any aspect of herself she desired. Carole took hold of her artistic abilities and developed them further than she'd dared before. She began exploring her whimsy and took up collecting the miniature art pieces that became the beginnings of the collection now housed in our Museum of Miniatures.

You can also take hold of your life at any point, at any age. You can change your perspective, reinvent yourself, find new aspects or depths of yourself and indulge them at any time. You can also rid yourself of those things you thought you were stuck with. It's simply a matter of accepting that you can, and wanting to. And those two things—accepting and wanting—need not diminish with age. They are available to you at any time, at any point in your life.

I met a woman named Penny on a cruise from Florida. She was a most interesting woman with a zest for life, a real joie de vivre. She told me that she had brought thirty changes of clothing with her, a different outfit for morning, afternoon, and evening; for sport, casual, formal, and informal occasions. Each change of clothes, she explained to me, reflected her mood, the mood she wished to present. The "looks" she assembled weren't intended so much for how others saw her, but for how she saw herself. She wanted to feel good about herself, and the changes in her appearance helped her do so. She seemed fresh and vital and renewed every time I ran across her. I could see in her eyes and bearing and face the pleasure she derived from her presentation.

Penny illustrated perfectly how change can enliven a person and how easy it can be to initiate refreshing changes. All she had to do was select a new outfit to make a new statement about her state of mind at the time.

You can do the same thing in any number of ways. Whether you change clothes or change the spelling of your name, opening yourself to new possibilities will let you forever renew your sense of joy and wonder at the goodness and wealth of life.

Georgette Mosbacher said in her recent book, *Feminine Force*,* "I'm not an extraordinary woman, but I'm a woman who has done some extraordinary things. I wasn't born beautiful, but I made myself as beautiful as I can be. I was an average student, who often learned lessons the hard way. I wasn't born to privilege, but I was privileged to be born to a family whose values strengthened me and equipped me to face the challenges of life. I suffered in an emotionally and physically abusive marriage, yet I've also managed to prosper, flourish, and survive."

You are what you make yourself into, what you choose to be. And you can make that choice at any time. You do not have to pick one path and never stray from it, you may branch off at any time. It's your life, and you may take it wherever you please. From any level you can make yourself into the best you can possibly be if you want it badly enough. All you have to do is release the power you hold within yourself to create the life you deserve. If your ship doesn't come in, swim out to it.

*Simon & Schuster—New York, NY. 1993.

Among Ms. Mosbacher's "72 Feminine Force Principles" are the following that I think are especially pertinent:

- I achieve success by not accepting failure.
- When I look my personal best, I am powerful.
- I will not love a [person] who does not cherish me.
- Regardless of the difficulties of my life, I will never become a victim.

Your life is a continuing journey. Its passage will not stop even if you sit still. Every moment that you are alive is another opportunity to become the person you most want to be. It is never too late. Remember, you only have one life, so live it while you can. Don't deny yourself the full expression of everything that is you.

It is a shame that too often a life is missed, actually lost, before it's over. It has been shown over and over again that many major successes happen after one reaches sixty-five. Don't fret about the inevitable arrival of your final destination, enjoy the ongoing journey. The happiest people I know are the ones who have come to realize that their satisfaction and gratification come from making the journey, from trying new things, from indulging new desires, from pursuing new goals. The destination is simply a method of keeping score (see Appendix 5).

As you get older, don't stop working. Start working. The happiest people I know in their eighties are those who are busy, who are indulging their interests. Who *live*! Dr. Robert Schuller, when told that people hoped he would accomplish everything he wanted to by the time he died, replied, "I hope not, for then I would have been dead, even before I died." Achievement and accomplishment are ongoing. If you accomplish everything you want to before you die, you will be dead before you die.

Living rich is a series of adjustments, as is life. However, you can control and change whatever doesn't suit you at any time. Remember, often you do whatever you do only because of a habit you have formed. Be patient with yourself and you can change those habits. If you commit yourself to a new idea or concept and implement those changes over a period of fifteen, thirty, or forty-five days, you'll find that the changes will quite effortlessly become new habits that offer fresh, vital new ways of seeing and doing things. What is a few weeks or months in the scope of your life? A solitary moment. A single breath. And what purpose does that time serve anyway if it is only used to preserve the habitual practice of things that do not sustain joy? Better to die in the process of embracing change and seeking satisfaction than to live in stagnation and mirthlessness.

What you think about, you can bring about. Build belief in a new set of goals. Write them out, picture them, imagine them, act as if they had already happened. Talk to yourself, over and over. Think of it as simply reprogramming your computer. The original computer, that is—your mind. Computer aficionados say, "Garbage in, garbage out," meaning that if you initiate a process incorrectly it will proceed incorrectly; if you feed in faulty data, you will receive a flawed conclusion. In human terms, I restate it as, "Negative thinking in, negative results out," the converse of which is true also: Positive thinking in, positive results out.

Wake up in the morning and say out loud, "I intend to be happy today." Resolve it, and you can be it, regardless of anything else that you might imagine is happening to affect your state of mind. It is *your* mind and you get to determine its state. Of course, you can be miserable if you make that choice. It is truly and simply up to you. People really can be as happy as they choose to be.

Without a functioning battery, your watch fails to operate, your radio, flashlight, notebook computer, and calculator all die. A new charge, energy, must come from a new battery when the time comes for the old one to be replaced. Put in an inefficient battery and your equipment will run inefficiently. Put in a dead battery and there will be no life. But put in a new, energy-filled battery and there will be an instant response. The vitality of the battery will determine the life of your equipment. It's no different for you. Replace your old, negative battery with a fresh, positive one and program yourself to produce whatever you want. Why make it more complicated than it is? You want to be happy. You want your life to be full. You want to surround yourself with people who love you and those that you love. Then do so. Make up your mind, embrace the desire, plan to succeed at what you desire, and do so. Just like that. What you want, you can have, if you'll only want it badly enough and pursue it tirelessly enough. What can you do better with your time, anyway? What could be more important than dedicating yourself to going after that which you most want out of life?

Do you think that it is possible to give love and not receive it in return? Do you think you can talk to people, asking them questions and listening to them, without their responding in kind, asking similar questions and spending similar time listening to you? If you are close to someone, do you think you can say, "I love you," without getting a similar response? If these moments give you pleasure, why wouldn't you initiate this response? Why wouldn't you surround yourself with all the possible happiness you can enjoy by simply bringing it about yourself? Don't look for others to make things happen for you. Don't rely on habits and rituals to supply what you need. Lead the way. Say it, see it, simulate it, picture it as if it already happened. It can be yours. It is all in your mind-set, and success is nothing more than a state of mind. At the expense of being totally redundant, but within the confines of my own philosophy of inundate and overkill: Believe you can do something and you will.

Do not procrastinate, do not wait; there will never be a more propitious time than now. Don't wait for tomorrow, for tomorrow never comes. Tomorrow is always today, and if you wait to act thinking that circumstances will be better tomorrow, you will be waiting for a time that never arrives.

If you have one more "I love you" inside you before you go to bed—let it out. Say it now just in case you have no tomorrow.

Let your desire and your motivation, your spirit and your will be born anew each day. Kick free of the chains of habit and fear that hold you to anything less than everything you want your life to be.

If Not Now, When?

You come first. If you are not satisfied, how can you satisfy anyone else? You *must* come first. You and your spouse are entitled to enjoy the rest of your lives, to delight in life every moment you can.

I truly and completely believe that there is no finer estate-planning tool, no better method for discounting the tremendous burden of the estate-tax costs wealthy people bear, than the leverage of life insurance placed within an irrevocable trust. There is no better means of optimizing and maximizing your assets for your heirs, no better buy for providing financial security.

Yet even so, the very first thing I tell any prospect who comes to me is that if paying for the policy will in any way diminish your own lifestyle, if it will in any way limit your own pleasures, *you should not do it*. I say this in my seminars, I say it in my books, I say it to clients in my office. Do not, I admonish them, provide for your posterity at the expense of yourself. Life, fleeting and precious, is for living first.

Rhonda wrote this poem about the importance of living each day fully and to your own satisfaction:

This is my life of which we speak—
No game or test of will from which to emerge
  victorious.
Death is no reward
For a lifetime of lessons and tallies on the slate.

This is my life.
Which, ending to beginning, in no more than
An instance without consequence.
And when it is over and my essence has departed unto
  the mysteries,
It will make no matter if I "won" or "lost";
There is no salvation where there is no life to save.

This is my only life—
So do not ask of me that I relinquish my glories;
That I trim my desires
To solve a puzzle wrought by someone else's hand.
Impose not your dreams on me; expect not your
  wishes to be mine.

This is my life.
And it will end before I know it has started.
There is no guarantee of time enough to answer all
  your wants of me
And have remembered pleasures of my own.
There is no right in beating back my nature to
  cultivate a garden
Fate may deny its bloom.

This is my life of which I speak—
Less than perfect I was created
And less than perfect 'tis my nature to be.
I will not spend what moments I've been given
In struggle for a Truth whose proof I'll never see
And I'll embrace what set of Truths that answers life
    for me.

Time is not a commodity to be brokered. It is not a theory that can be bent by statistics into whatever form we choose. Forget about the odds and mortality rates that suggest you have a given amount of time. They are all wrong. Time, as it is applied to any specific individual, exists outside all rules and law. It cannot be contained or predicted. So you must alter your relationship to it. You must put yourself first, claim your time for your own, with the awareness that each moment could be your last. Make the plans you need to make for what you will leave behind, but do not live for those posthumous plans.

Live for each day, for yourself, and then you can live better for those you love.

First and foremost, try to stop thinking about life in terms of the things you *have* to do, and try thinking in terms of the things you *want* to do. What would you regret not having done if you were to find out tomorrow you had an incurable disease? And what are you waiting for in pursuing that goal or dream? Time makes no promise that it will wait with you.

Of course, life makes demands of all of us. We need to earn money in order to have food and shelter, and we are not truly free to simply go through each day doing only that which we feel like doing. Our families need us, our friends need us, and being a member of a society and a community requires that we not always think strictly about ourselves.

But there is not a single person I have talked to in the last several months while I've been formulating the text for this book who does not admit to having some intention of doing something that he is waiting to begin. Taking a class, a trip, reconciling with an estranged friend or family member, starting a creative project, getting fit or losing weight. As far as I can tell, *all* people have these notions in mind. But many, if not most, speak of doing these things "later" or "soon," assuming that there will be a soon or a later; that time will accommodate them. Tragedies strike everywhere, all the time.

I remember, when I heard about the accident that actor Christopher Reeve suffered, how frightened and dismayed I felt. I wondered about my reaction. Surely what happened to him was horrible and tragic, but why, I wondered, should it strike me as being worse just because he was famous? After all, I don't know him personally, my life is no more affected by his hardship than by the myriad of anonymous others who suffer similar disasters every day. Why does his plight provoke such grief?

The answer I finally found was that we all yearn for some concept of safety in life. We all want to believe that there is some attainable place where we will be immune from the random strikes of life's cruelties. If we can only amass money or build up our bodies to be strong and healthy or become famous and respected, we will be safe from hardship, illness, loneliness, loss. Then, when we see that tragedy strikes even those people who have achieved that place, who have the money, fame, and physical strength that we mistakenly believed protects them from the dire fates of more ordinary people, we know there is no safe place, no escape from time's whimsy.

It's a scary thought. But also, I hope, a motivating one.

Don't count on time as an ally. It is not necessarily on your side. "If not now, when?" The question was first posed by Hillel the elder around 30 B.C. If not now, when?

Your whole life is just a series of "nows" strung together. The past is done and behind you. It had impact on getting you where you are today, and looking back to it you can learn things and see how progressions occurred. But that doesn't change the present. The future, having not yet occurred, makes no promise that it will. Ultimately, **_now_** is it. **_Now_** is all you really have.

The same applies to those you love and care about. Time is wild and uncontrollable for them, too. Which, if you think about it, is an even scarier thought than that of your own mortality.

If I contemplate leaving something undone, missing out on some experience I wanted to have, I find some comfort, strange as it may seem, in the knowledge that once I have died I'll be released from the sense of regret or yearning. But if I think about the people closest to me leaving or dying with unfinished things between us, I realize that I will have to live the rest of my life with the knowledge that things can never be fixed or repaired. My regret will stay with me as long as I live.

How tragic it is when people forget that time does not promise time *enough*. When they operate on the assumption of a tomorrow that winds up never coming. Tell the people you love that you love them today. Make peace now with the people you know you will eventually make peace with.

Here's an exercise you can do to help you focus on your relationship with time. Make a list of the people in your life: your family, friends, coworkers, associates. Now go through it and imagine that each person on it suddenly died. Does it seem a gruesome undertaking? If it does, it's probably because you would prefer not to think about the reality of death. But death *is* a reality, and those people can and will die. You have no control over that fact, which is why so many people avoid thinking about it. But you do have control over how you accept that fact into your life.

If someone on your list were to die, you would naturally miss that person and grieve his or her passing and feel bad for the things he or she left behind unfinished. But are there individuals on your list for whom you would feel other things? Is there the panicked pang of unresolved business associated with the thought of losing someone you know? If so, what are you waiting for? Do you want to live the rest of your life with that feeling forever associated with that person's memory? If you don't do something about it now, then when? Tomorrow? There is no tomorrow.

I tell my wife I love her every day. I buy her gifts or do special things for her whenever the feeling strikes—I do not wait for predetermined occasions. I let the people I care about know it all the time, for I would be loath for them to die without my having told them what they meant to me. In the same way, it troubles me to imagine that I might die having never said the words that might help sustain them.

And I am aware of the other side of time as well. That my life is not over until it's over. I think there is little that is sadder than people who reach a certain point in their lives and basically stop living and start dying. I am now sixty-seven years old. I have completed the writing of this, my fourth book, and have only recently opened, along with my wife, our Museum of Miniatures. I have already planned my next two books, *Die Rich 2*, and, if this one is successful, *Live Rich 2*, after which I hope to tackle my autobiography. New business ventures come my way every day. And I stay young from the excitement and the activity. It is never too late to enrich your life. There are things you can do at any age, in any condition of finances or health that will engage your mind and your imagination and your spirit. Things to challenge and amuse you; things to bring you joy.

Don't surrender to time a single second before you have to. Live every moment that you can.

Maybe it is working in this industry, helping people be prepared for death, that has so focused my sense of time. Whatever the genesis, I learned long ago that the only thing I can count on when it comes to time is my own capacity to relish it and my own willingness to embrace its randomness and unpredictability. And I am very grateful that I learned the lessons when I did. If I hadn't, I might now be carrying around guilt and regret and unhappiness over having left things undone. My life would have been robbed of some of its richness by the self-recriminations I would be stuck with.

Below is the first stanza of a poem written by Rhonda about two lovers whom fate is separating, probably forever.

Time is not a line
Marching stoically through the days
An arrow straight procession
From the past to what's to be.
Time knows no steady measure
No imposed regularity
Conceived to serve as reference
Amidst the randomness and chaos.
Time changes with perception.
Sweeps by or crawls pitifully
As a heartbeat pounds or wavers
And breath quickens or is held. . . .

The poem concludes:

So do not weep, beloved,
For we are together, forever
Right now.

It's true. Each moment as it occurs embodies a whole forever within it, the way each cell in the body contains the map
for the whole person. Once passed, it cannot be changed; it
remains indelible.

To live rich it is important that you recognize the true
nature of time so that you can seize your life each and every
day. Put things off until a tomorrow that may never come—
whether they are things you want to do or things you need
to express or resolve about your relationship with someone—and you risk existing within a "never" that is the very
embodiment of an impoverished spirit.

There is a song written by Albert Hammond and John
Bettis entitled "One Moment in Time."* Even without the
music it should make your heart sing. I could want no more
appropriate words to conclude my message of living rich by
living *now*.

Each day I live
I want to be a day to give
The best of me.
I'm only one,
But not alone,
My finest day is yet unknown.
I broke my heart for every gain,
To taste the sweet I've faced the pain.
I rise and fall,
Yet through it all,

*Reprinted by permission of Warner/Chappell Music—Los Angeles, CA.

This much remains,
I want one moment in time.

When I'm more than I thought I could be,
When all my dreams are a heartbeat away and
The answers are all up to me,
Give me one moment in time.
When I'm racing with destiny,
Then in that one moment of time,
I will feel,
I will feel eternity.

I live to be the very best.
I want it all,
No time for less.
I've laid my plans,
Now lay the chance,
Here in my hands.
Give me one moment in time.

You're a winner for a lifetime,
If you seize that one moment in time,
Make it shine.
Give me one moment in time,
When I'm more than I thought I could be,
When all of my dreams
Are a heartbeat away
And the answers are all up to me.

Give me one moment in time,
When I'm racing with destiny,
Then in that one moment of time,
I will be,
I will be free,
I will be free.

If your moment is not now, when?

18

The More You Give Away, the More You Receive

I don't think it's possible for a richly lived life to be a selfishly lived life. We are all members of a community, a society, a species. It is in our nature to bond with others, to share mutual concerns. And I think that in the long run we can better things for ourselves only by helping to better them for everyone.

An old English proverb reads: "He who has no charity, deserves no mercy." And a true measure of your worth includes all the benefits others have gained from your success.

Eric Hopper, speaking on the same subject, said, "We probably have a greater love for those we support than for those who support us. Our vanity carries more weight than our self-interest."

The relationship of a single man with his fellow men has been a topic of reflection since the beginning of time. Aristotle said, "The unfortunate need people who will be kind to them;

the prosperous need people to be kind to.'' None of us lives in a vacuum. We are part of a greater whole, and only by recognizing and embracing this concept can we satisfy the need that exists within us for membership and society. We need to reverse the trend of isolation and solitary pursuit that has been our response to our fears about the strangeness and dangers and life, and instead work together and share ourselves. For this is how accord is reached. This is how the barriers that separate people from one another are toppled.

Many people don't know their hearts are closed until they open them. Open yourself to the world that is around you. Use due caution, of course, but within the boundaries of your physical safety extend yourself to the people around you. Look them in the eye and let your own eye reflect your goodwill and desire to find and issue acceptance. Give of yourself in every way that you can. You will be amazed at what you get back.

You must give away something if you want to receive anything. And you must communicate. Whether the conversation is between the representatives of two countries or two individuals—including a married couple—you must talk to each other, give words to the feelings, give voice to the needs. Share your thoughts and desires. For without communication, there can be no understanding, mending, or reconciliation.

In 1977, at Ben-Gurion University in Beer Sheva, a historic peace treaty was signed by Israeli Prime Minister Menachem Begin and Egyptian President Anwar Sadat. I felt both humbled and awed to know that signing was taking place on the Carol and Barry Kaye Mall, the result of a donation I had made in 1976 in thanks to God for what he has made possible for my family and me.

Little happened to further the peace these two men had

pioneered until, in 1994, PLO leader Yasser Arafat shook hands with Yitzhak Rabin and forged the beginnings of a new Middle East peace. There could be no peace for the world without the dialogues these brave men initiated. Someone must speak to someone else. The warring factions must discuss their needs, must barter and compromise and give in order to receive.

The hatred and intolerance and mistrust in any situation can be resolved only through discussion. Only a meeting of the minds, a verbal give and take, a summit to promote mutual understanding will provide the foundation upon which stable relations can be built.

The same is true on a personal level. You too must communicate, compromise, barter, and give of yourself in order to receive.

Franklin Roosevelt once said, "Human kindness has never weakened the stamina or softened the fiber of a free people. A nation does not have to be cruel to be tough." More important, an individual does not have to be cruel in order to prove who he is. Ralph Sockman said it this way: "Nothing is so strong as gentleness, and nothing is so gentle as real strength."

Give, and you shall receive. When you put yourself out there and open yourself to life, you are rewarded with all manner of delights. People will desire to be with you, they will share themselves and go out of their way on your behalf. The more of yourself you share, the more of yourself you find. You can only be fulfilled if you share. What good is fulfillment if you can't share it with someone else? As you open up to others, you achieve access to them as well, and you can start to perceive your own value and worth as they perceive it in you. It is said that your luck is how you treat people. Take this under advisement. Remember that you have not lived a perfect day, even though you have earned your money, unless you have done something for someone without any expectation that they will repay you. The contemporary way of spreading this message is found on bumper stickers across the country that encourage people to "practice senseless acts of beauty and random kindness," an expression that was coined in opposition to the dishearteningly constant news of "random, senseless acts of violence." Fighting against despair in their own, small, singular ways, individuals can make a difference. Remember in your dealing with people from day to day that "the giving is the hardest part; what does it cost to add a smile?"

Sarah Bernhardt said, "Life begets life. Energy creates energy. It is only by spending one's self that one becomes rich."

Some of the greatest joys and most rewarding experiences I have had have centered around my charitable or philanthropic activities. There is a sense of expanding myself, of growing larger and more vital, that I derive from my participation in good works.

We live in a very materialistic society where personal worth is most often measured in dollars and assets. As a result, we tend to think of the amassing of goods and money as the primary determinant of a richly lived life. But giving, in my experience, nets a greater return than getting.

The rewards of a charitable outlook are many. In a way, it seems odd to discuss them; we're raised to think of being charitable as something you do for others without thought for yourself. To speak of the benefits we derive in any terms other than a religious/spiritual context can seem, at first, to diminish the act. Making it about what we get, as opposed to what we give, seems contrary to the intended spirit.

But I don't believe in pure altruism; I don't think it exists. At some level we all make our choices of behavior and attitude and action because those choices support some need within us. Even Mother Teresa, I am sure, likes what she is doing and feels her own life is enriched by following the course she has chosen for herself.

So there is nothing wrong with evaluating the benefits of a charitable endeavor in terms of what we receive by engaging in it. It does not diminish the giving one bit to admit and accept that we get something for it—something tangible and worthwhile—in return, even if it is only recognition or public relations. The goods and services are no less valuable to those who need them, the donated facilities are no less utilized, the time spent helping others is no less needed, for the fact that you received something, some great personal satisfaction, in exchange.

The person you really help most is yourself. You don't exist separately from the community of your family, friends, peers, and associates. Their welfare affects your own. If their streets are unsafe, so are yours. If their teenagers are joining gangs, yours are also in danger. Will business come to you if your neighborhood deteriorates, if your customers become impoverished? This is the joy of giving: It comes back around, making a united circle of people linked together, struggling and surviving and overcoming the common hardships that, when they affect one person in the circle, ultimately affect us all. Everything you do to support the infrastructure of society, to elevate humanity, to help provide comfort and care, also supports, elevates, and provides for you.

On a more individual or personal level, giving can be an even greater reward.

There is so much a person can do to help better the world for himself and others. Charitable giving need not be in the form of money. Your time and effort and creative skills are as valuable as your cash. I believe *everyone* has something to give that will help.

Who does not have a few hours a week they usually spend sitting in front of the television set that they could be using to be a big brother or sister, or to work at their church or synagogue or volunteer at the hospital? Who is so without any single skill they could not teach or share with others? The list of needed services is virtually endless, the ways you can make a difference in other lives infinite. Do these things— read to the sick or elderly, supervise a course at the YMCA, be a big brother or sister to a troubled child, visit the elderly at a nursing home, join the campaign for a cause you believe in—and you will find your life greatly enriched. Support a political candidate whom you think can make a difference. You will meet the kind of people who share your ideals or you'll unlock something inside yourself that enhances your appeal. Most important, you will receive a sense of satisfaction beyond anything you can imagine.

I knew of a young woman who was extremely shy. At parties and other get-togethers she tended to sit alone, watching. She smiled pleasantly and was an attractive person, but her discomfort showed and it made others uncomfortable around her. She desired to be in a relationship but despaired that she would ever be able to put herself forth enough to find someone.

There was one area, however, in which this woman shined. She loved children. She felt safe with them and let her nurturing, imaginative side show through. At family-oriented events she could always be found in the midst of a circle of children, laughing with them, telling a story, or simply sitting patiently while the little girls played with her long hair. She was beautiful at those times.

After trying dating services and personal ads, blind dates

arranged by friends, and social functions, the woman had basically given up on finding a love interest for herself. To ease the hurt and the loneliness, she volunteered in the children's ward of her local hospital. It made her feel needed and gave her an outlet for her love. And the children loved her! She'd read to them and act out all the characters, unconcerned in their innocent company for whether or not she looked silly. She'd sing to them when they were scared and having trouble sleeping, hold their hands when they were in pain.

One day, one of the little girls on the floor was going in for surgery. As was her habit, the young woman, whose volunteer shift had ended, stayed in the hospital and waited for the surgery to conclude and to know that the child was safe. Before leaving, she made sure the little girl had her favorite stuffed animal nearby when she awoke.

The next day, the young woman was approached in the hallway by a nice-looking man. Instantly she was shy and nervous, not making eye contact, mumbling and fidgety.

"I wanted to thank you," the man said, undeterred by her distance. "Marcy [the little girl] is my daughter. You've helped her so much."

The young woman blushed and stammered a thank-you.

"The thing is," the man proceeded, "I've seen you with the kids when I've been here to visit Marcy. You're wonderful with them and I, well, you obviously have such a good heart and you're funny and imaginative and I was wondering, I'm a widower, and I was wondering if you'd like to go out with me sometime."

Though apprehensive and unsure, the young woman agreed; to this day she cannot tell me why or what it was about the man that made her willing to take the risk. They dated for about a year and were married three years ago.

Give, and you will receive. The thing this young woman wanted most came to her as a direct result of the opening of her heart to others.

Give, and you will receive. Extend yourself beyond yourself and the things you cherish and desire most from life will be drawn toward you. What more rich an existence could you ever envision?

Go live a rich life. Then share those riches of spirit, heart, mind, and pocketbook, and watch them multiply exponentially.

IT WORKED
FOR HER

A t the beginning of this book, you were shown how the systems, ideas, and philosophies included in this book worked to make my life a rich and fulfilling one. Then you were promised that those same methods, motivations, and concepts could work for you in helping you to enrich your own life. A wonderful example of the power of that promise happened before the book was even finished.

After all the initial meetings and discussions were over, after the outline had been formulated and the contents determined, I delivered *Live Rich* into Rhonda's capable hands for the preparation of the manuscript's first draft and went about addressing the myriad other demands made on my time. With so much happening in the world and in my life, it was some time before I surfaced again to wonder what had become of the book; it was not like Rhonda to be late, yet I hadn't heard from her and it was, I noted with some surprise, past the appointed date when we were to reconvene.

I reached her on the phone and asked why I hadn't heard from her yet. Somewhat abashed, yet not altogether apologetic, she said, "Well, Barry, the truth is, I've been focusing on other things. You weren't pushing so, admittedly, I didn't push either."

I was a bit miffed, but knowing Rhonda as I do, I was more intrigued as to what could keep her from upholding an obligation.

"Some time ago," she explained in answer to my inquiry, "I had an idea for a business. But I put it on the shelf; I was unsure of its merit, somewhat afraid to pursue it and to risk the money and personal investment required to make it happen. It's nagged at me from time to time but I haven't listened.

"Then, well, this may sound corny, but as I was working on *Live Rich*, I began to feel some anxiety about not doing all I could to make my idea a reality. I guess you could say, Barry, that I started to *really* listen to what you were saying and it made an impression. I simply couldn't wait anymore. So I've been spending a lot of time putting the business together these past weeks—time I should have been devoting to *Live Rich*."

How could I be angry? She sounded so excited, and what's more, she had unintentionally provided me with the greatest validation imaginable of the power of my *Live Rich* philosophies and methods.

In six weeks, Rhonda had taken an idea for a project she had dreamed of "one day" enacting and made it happen. She'd formed a corporation, raised the initial money, and put together all the required business necessities. Her idea to produce and market a videotape that would teach people how to perform emergency first aid on their dogs was being realized, and K-911, Incorporated, was born. She'd written the script for the video, and all the pricing and general information was completed for her 800 telephone number service. She had applied for and received bank approval to take credit card orders over the phone. She had a production company lined up to film the video, arrangements made for back-end fulfillment, and advertising ready to be put in place. It was a remarkable feat made doubly so by the quickness and certainty with which she'd acted.

"I don't know what I was waiting for," she said as we discussed her accomplishment. "I guess I was hoping someone would come along and do it for me. Or maybe I wanted some guarantee that it would all work out all right. But as I was writing, the words started to penetrate beyond my brain and into my heart. I started being more afraid of *not* proceeding than of going ahead. What if someone else beat me to it? That would be so awful. To think I'd had the idea and the ability and the resources and had simply let the opportunity go out of fear or lack of belief in myself. It felt terrible."

Now Rhonda's company is well on its way to a much-deserved success. Her K-911 Emergency First Aid video is produced, and it's good! She is being met with favorable responses all over the pet-care and pet-products industries. More important, she is infused with a new sense of purpose. However much she enjoys and excels at the writing she has done for me and others, this project is *hers*! It's an expression of her love and concern for animals, a real opportunity for her to utilize all her skills and abilities, a source of enormous pride for a job well done. And it offers her a greater reward in terms of both personal and financial fulfillment.

Rhonda can now be said to truly be living rich. She dared a dream and is making it a reality. Every day, as K-911 grows and meets with new success and approval, her sense of herself grows along with it. She rejected the control that fear had on her life and embraced risk to avoid regret. She decided not to wait in the hope that life would eventually offer up the rewards she desired; instead she grabbed for them now. She found something she loved and became imbued with the energy to pursue it relentlessly.

The Live Rich philosophies contained in this book worked for me; they were the foundation upon which all my personal and professional success has been built. They have now worked for Rhonda; she credited her work on this project as having provided the inspiration and impetus for her to strike out bravely and with great determination upon the road to her dream. I believe they can do the same for you. I believe anyone with the desire, the drive, and the willingness to dare can have a rich life, a life filled with the unique pleasure and joy of potential realized, of ambition sated, of dreams come true.

APPENDICES

One night, when he was fourteen years old, Barry Kaye was compelled by a profound burst of creative insight to pen the following expressions of his personal philosophy. Reflecting the enthusiasm, optimism, and strength of purpose that infused his vision of the world, these pieces rushed from his heart onto the paper in a single magical night. He has not composed anything quite like them since. But the power of that night has stayed him, as has the truth that is expressed in each piece. They became the foundation of his entire approach to living and life, the impetus that carried him forward into a rich and satisfying life. Enjoy them for further understanding and your own utilization.

Appendix One

THEN THIS I SAY
ON SOCIETY
1942

As I sit here at this ungodly hour in a position so uncouth that it truly does subdue my real character, I stop a bit to pan, to think of all the world so great in relation to I the human being.

Can it be that this man speaks seriously when thoughts and deeds too unexplainable for groups who grope among the darkest inner thoughts are prone in situation same to conquer man's inadequate excuses for reasoning?

Then truly I ask, though knowing, why must I withhold my desire for that that isn't and cannot be, due to a group sufficiently equipped, I say, with bow and staff to meet the oncoming horde of fire and blast, steel and shell though created by man's agile mind too weak to combat the instruments that he did forge. This I say, with all due disrespect, for man who had made for himself, though be I alone, a symbol that is the exemplification of nothing. I alone, then must be.

A failure in sight, so plainly undisguised, that to attack and tear apart would be as the lion stalking his prey, the lamb, who innocently below awaits the day to pass him by so that once again upon the newborn sun he may take up his labors that died with the falling of the sun, to await the day that passes by.

Then this I say, in answer to my thoughts, it is seriously that I do speak. If within the pencil, one can find the answer to a thought that pierces body, soul, and mind, then it is I you see who stands upon the hill bared by man yet clinging to nature still though her elements now at work act as a slap across the face.

But, if in the final stage we derive this, I am right, then still in vain I know it shall be won, for the winning is in a vacuum that is sealed in such a way that but the final stroke can penetrate and this I know can never be.

So broken, bent perhaps, according to the wish, still I'll buy my chain and ever keep it free for the ball that must in the end hold, shall never, I do pray, shackle me.

Appendix Two

THEN THIS I SAY
ON THOUGHTS
1942

If I were to stop and think, what thoughts divine would enter my small, way-too-simple mind? That is if I could think, and think I can, and will, and do, for thoughts are my company.

I think about things so little and find, in amazement I might add, that it is I and not the thoughts so contained that make it take the feeling small. Then at times of things great I'll think and baffled be, by their many intricacies, then laugh to find that it is only I these puzzles form.

My companions, I do perceive, are tests that after done never wander or do stray but instead remain for only me within my consciousness. Then I must choose my thoughts with great discretion and at all times remain aloof to desires that may with the passing of the time reveal themselves to be malignant thoughts, twisting, squirming, even winning out before the curtain falls, thus staining company and peace of mind.

Someday perhaps, when finally I am free, I'll release my comrades in words so expressed, that will be like the walking of a man with legs that don't, or the seeing of a man with eyes that can't, and then I shall know that companions remain as such only when suppressed and as such are far better still then running free and wild. For never were intended, thoughts to be, but thoughts to remain within one's own and never be released. For let them fall and no longer still, a lonely stranger, can they give company.

But if this expression, I desire, and I do as surely as a thought I can think, then take pity, for there stands before you a man that must in all eventuality be torn apart and taught to think in conformity.

Then so it will, but I must state, that not the line can hold or bind for inwardly I shall always find a new companion waiting there for me.

APPENDIX THREE

THEN THIS I SAY
ON HOME
1942

My own, a feeling not a place, that's my home. To me as you, it would seem the same, no matter where. It's the place I want to be, and be I will, always there.

Possess I must, that feeling that lives surely with us all, for then that upon my life, is based. Then I must say my home is me and it I make. And live I must within the realm conceived by me and for my very own.

Then how shall I make my home and in what position shall it be? On what foundation shall I build and of what material must it consist? Shall I strive for big or small or just contented be, to add as I grow into its needs? Then it would seem I say, that as my house does grow so shall I, and in turn as I attain, then in my home that attainment you will find.

Therefore it's not for me to spring and advantage take of movement by leaps and bounds, for then hollow my house will be, acting as a mere pretense, an empty shell. And if I should call upon my house, as a rubber tapper upon his tree, there would be no sap waiting there to be tapped by me. In case described, my walls would crumble and in ruin, at my feet they would lie, near their foundation that in the shuffle and frenzied pace was not built.

What has happened to my feeling? Where does my home now stand? What has happened to my place? Clearly then, without review, the realization is now within my grasp. The built is in the building and the building in my hands still remains.

Then how shall I build my house? With body strong, molded and steadfast from consistency. And what shall its position be? A progressive one indeed, that grows with time a certainty upon which I may be insured a self-needed form of dependency.

From that foundation strongly raised and so entrenched, there will grow as only growth there can exist through efforts mine, a home, not a place, but a feeling stout and firm. Then this without fear of reproach, I may call my own.

APPENDIX FOUR

THEN THIS I SAY
ON DECISIONS

1942

A decision is in the making, but which way shall I decide? Shall I find it right or wrong, shall I be pro or con? In turning, which way shall it be?

Then quickly, as time is short, as short as time, I must stop my procrastination, a decision must be forthcoming. If in the choosing I should see a way that's wrong, as wrong can be, what then will be my plight? How shall this affect my being? This mistake, that I might use, in reference to, will its cost be light or in direct contrast, too heavy for me alone the burden bear? Then truly, it does seem, a grave responsibility to my fellow man no matter how small or in content personal, my decision is to be.

In every instance, no matter what the case, a decisive move must be taken, be it the line after next from my pen or the step upon which a future's fate may hang. Then deliberate thinking, planning at length, must be given if I am not to stray.

So after careful consideration, of mind, of heart, and on my tongue is plainly spelled an answer as if to a long, drawn-out puzzle, which truly is, I'll think once again, again review for later peace of mind. For once done, all and more will not recall and then nothing can undo.

But to tear apart, it would seem, this theory, wrong for once I choose, no matter, I have chosen right, for whose decision but my own places a thing in right or wrong, so surely my selection must be correct or during judgment still, I would have found the faults and points and picked for right what now I have chosen wrong. But either way my preference still is of perfection for I must have chosen what I felt best.

The decision then is in the thinking. And as such, it stands my thoughts may be judged right or wrong, but never my decision, for then too late.

Appendix Five

THEN THIS I SAY
ON LIFE AND TRUTH
1942

The years have passed and now . . . too late . . . or yet too soon . . . for all is never over . . . and everything has yet to begin. Then each ending becomes a new beginning and each find leads to a new search . . . never old always new. There is no Now . . . it's before and after . . . even then and when but never here. Satisfaction is in expectation . . . gratification again brings need . . . and need is constant. The exquisite test is release and this is never known . . . answers unquestioned . . . desire insatiable for peace and quiet . . . tranquil sweet calm too still . . . unmoving . . . for understanding in our time.

APPENDIX SIX

Returning to the typewriter fifty-four years after he wrote the five preceding articles which comprise his *Then This I Say* series, Barry Kaye closed the circle of his remarkable vision with the following piece. In aggregate, the body of his work, including this book, now extends itself through the need, the process, and the reward of living a rich life.

THEN THIS I SAY ON LIVING RICH

1 9 9 6

To love and be loved
To live every moment to its fullest
To be happy—to spread joy
To hurt no one, to help everyone
To see—to breathe, to feel—to realize
To be sensitive to each scent—every touch
To know and grow and show.

What is life, if not to live.
And what is joy, if not to give
You are indeed rich
If you are there for all
Then it can be truly said
Here is one, who lived the richest
With every fiber of one's being
With all and more, and no regret
This ONE truly did
LIVE RICH.

Index